# TWO RAVENS

# TWO RAVENS

## The Life and Teachings of a Spiritual Warrior

Louis Two Ravens Irwin
and
Robert Liebert

Destiny Books
Rochester, Vermont

Destiny Books
One Park Street
Rochester, Vermont 05767
Web Site: http://www.gotoit.com

LIBRARY OF CONGRESS CATALOGING-IN-PUBLICATION DATA

Irwin, Louis Two Ravens, 1933–1995.
    Two Ravens : the life and teachings of a spiritual warrior /
  Louis Two Ravens Irwin and Robert Liebert.
      p.  cm.
    ISBN 0-89281-571-X
    1. Irwin, Louis Two Ravens, 1933–1995. 2. Siouan Indians—
Biography. 3. Siouan Indians—Religion. 4. Siouan Indians—
Politics and government. 5. Spiritual life—Great Plains. I.
Liebert, Robert M., 1956–    . II. Title.
    E99.S6175   1996
    978.004'975—dc20                                96-26097
                                                       CIP

Printed and bound in the United States

10  9  8  7  6  5  4  3  2

Text design and layout by Peri Champine
This book was typeset in Trump Mediaeval

Destiny Books is a division of Inner Traditions International

# CONTENTS

# ACKNOWLEDGMENTS

There are countless family members, elders, ancestors, and people in the Native American community—at the sundances, in the prisons, in the American Indian Movement, and indeed throughout the world—whom Louis would have liked to dedicate this book to. Louis and I had discussed a dedication that would read simply: *mitakuye oyasin*, to all my relations.

My thanks go out to: Daphne Irwin, Kenny Irwin, Donna Barrows, Dreke Irwin, John Irwin, Tony Mandan, Grandma Sadie, Steve Roubideau, Leonard Peltier, the Raisin clan, Ednah New Rider Weber, Valerian Three Irons, Archie Fire Lame Deer, Rick Thomas, and Jan Liebert.

I would also like to honor Louis's grandchildren: Molly Laurae, Johnna Tate, Joseph Byars, Jacinda Faye, Wolf Grass, Dakota, Patrice, and Biff.

# FOREWORD

## by Robert Liebert

This is the life story of a warrior. There are those who called Louis Two Ravens Irwin a Sun Dance chief and a medicine man, but Louie never called himself those things. For anyone that hung on his words he would launch into a long oratorical speech in the best Hollywood Indian tradition and end in his most serious tone with "I have spoken!" Then he would flash one of his famous smiles with that mischievous twinkle in his eyes, and you would know you'd been had. For Louie, and according to the Old Ways, no one was any holier than any other, and nothing could really be taught except that the truth was to be sought within. The closest thing he ever gave to advice consisted of two words: "Be real."

I believe, though, that he may have acknowledged himself as a warrior for his people and their ways. His training began with the things he was taught by his Arickara grandfather, who sent him into the Badlands at the age of twelve to survive and learn. All too soon Louis was thrust into the horrors of the Korean War at age seventeen. He was one of the youngest to fight, and returned with physical and emotional scars that remained with him throughout his life. He fought in the streets with the racism that is still rampant in this country. As a lifelong member of the American Indian Movement he traveled to many of the places where his people fought for their rights. He participated in the siege at Wounded Knee, the protests at Big Mountain, and in the Longest Walk. And toward the end of his days he fought hard for the release from prison of his spiritual brother Leonard Peltier. He fought to bring the sweat lodge and the practice of Native American spiritual ways to other prisons, for those who had little hope. Louie also held the vision that revived an ancient warrior society of his Mandan and Hidatsa people that had been extinct for eighty-six years. The Blackmouth Warrior Society acted as both the defenders and law keepers of the tribe. In addition to the Blackmouths' duties in seeing that respect was maintained during the sacred ceremonies of his people, Louis also saw their role as being more universal, as warriors who would fight to see that respect was maintained between all peoples.

Some of his greatest battles were inner ones; he knew all too well that a warrior's greatest enemy is the one within us. Anger at the white race, battles with alcohol, and shame for things he had done ate away at him. To find balance, Louie had to walk a difficult road back to the childhood teachings of his grandfather and of what Louie called: "the ways of the ways," the ancient teachings of how to find balance in this life. Much of what he regained he found through the Sun Dance ceremony, which had been banned for many years by the U.S. government.

Born at a time when his people still had their farms, their chiefs, and their spiritual ways, he grew up to see those things devastated with the damming of their beloved Missouri River. This and the many other things done to his race, and the fact that he had fought and killed and nearly given his own life in a white man's war, caused a deep bitterness and anger in Louie, and at a time when it was particularly bad to be a Native American in white society. Yet he overcame the anger to the degree that he could become, as he called it, "a bridge between cultures." He took the things he had learned and brought them to the wardens of the prisons and to his alcohol counseling, shared them with a small group of culturally and spiritually deprived whites and mixed-blood people whom he called his *tiyoshpaye*, his extended family, and spoke for the careful sharing of the sacred ways of the Red Road with all races. He became a warrior who spoke for peace and respect and balance.

Louis was also a bridge in another sense, in that his life bridged the time when his people still had much of their culture intact, through a time when Native Americans everywhere had lost pride in themselves, into an era of battles fought to regain their pride, their culture, and their land. Now that "Indian ways" have become popular, there are many, including the younger generation of Native Americans, that may not know about the struggles that were required to keep those ways alive within a dominant culture that was bent on destroying them.

Louie's patience was often tried by outsiders who came to him full of their own ideas or in a big hurry to learn Native American ways; yet he knew that in the true teachings of the Purification Lodge and the Sun Dance all things are related as the children of one Father and one Mother, and that those spiritual ways were not an "Indian way" but a way of being a human being, an "earth person." This doesn't mean that he believed that those of other races should take on the ceremonies of his people, but that the basic teachings were important to the survival of all.

These teachings he brought to his counseling, and many damaged people owe their recovery to Louie and his teachings. Louie combined the best of the white man's psychology with the best of his own people's. Mostly he knew how to get inside a person. Some of these teachings, taken from Louie's notes and his words, are found in the appendix "Walking the Sacred Circle." They are not the secrets of ancient rituals; they are ideas and practices he used to help those he counseled. I believe they are of great meaning to every one of us that seeks inner growth and the balance we have lost.

Those who are seeking a do-it-yourself guide to Native American rituals or the majestic visions of a New Age prophet will have to look elsewhere. The lessons here are simple but deep. Though Louie saw many miraculous healings and visions through the Sun Dance, the Purification Lodge, and the fast, those he wished to share were visions that he felt were given for "the People" as a whole. Among his traditional people the worth of a vision or powers is not in what honor or majesty they impart to the person, but in what they bring that may be of benefit to the People. "The People" is the name by which most Native tribes traditionally refer to themselves; in the modern usage of the Sun Dance Way, it has come to be used in a universal sense to include all of humanity. Many contemporary Native American writings emphasize the reverence we must hold toward the natural world; few speak as eloquently as Louis for what we can offer our fellow human beings, for what we can bring to an ever-expanding community of the People.

Louis knew that he could easily become a spiritual guru or a famous lecturer. He could tour the country making money running sweat lodges and initiating white people as others had done, but he was afraid for himself and afraid always that he would bring disgrace to his people. Instead, as a "bridge between cultures" Louie tried to teach non-Natives respect. He would say to us not to bring our books and our ideas to the Native people; not to add things or fragment the teachings, as was done with Christianity; not to come ready to take from the people, for there is the very real feeling that white people have taken everything else and now want their religion too. Instead, he would say, come to the Native people with a desire to know the culture first, make friends, help out with the work, and come ready to listen.

There is a powerful story here, and Louie wanted it told not to talk about the powers he was given or the famous people he has known, but to show the power of the Great Spirit in turning around the life of one pitiful human being, as we all are. I think most of all he wanted to share it with young Native Americans as an example of how they too could, with the help of the Creator, find balance and strength and pride in themselves, to inspire them to find and use the gifts they were given by the Creator.

There are many more stories that could be told of Louie, sad stories and stories that would bring tears of laughter, and those who knew him will agree that the whole story could never be told. Louie will have his detractors: those who knew him during his long bouts with alcohol, and those who even in his last years may have discovered that he was less than perfect, given to the same pitfalls and temptations as other people. He was the most *human* being I have known, and as complex as he was human. Within these pages are the things Louis chose to share.

In my own life Louie was the one who showed me a spiritual way to walk. He's the one who, when I crawled into the sweat lodge for the first time, made me know that with all the books I had read, I knew nothing until I knew it in my heart. I remember the time when I was on a fast in the rain and Louie came out to the woods at 3 A.M. to bring me a plastic tarp to cover myself. He was a man with a big heart who was still in the process of being healed, a man who loved to laugh and joke as few others could. As one of Louis's Sun Dance brothers said, "The Red Road can be a hard road to travel, and things are going to be a little harder now that Louie's gone."

AVA, MISSOURI
FIRST YEAR OF THE WHITE BUFFALO CALF

# Prologue:

# THE FLOOD

by Robert Liebert

*The flood of the wasichus, dirty with lies and
bad deeds, threatened to destroy the little
islands that were left to us.*

—FROM *BLACK ELK SPEAKS*

The people watched as the dirty brown waters rose slowly
but relentlessly. Not the raging spring torrent of Rocky
Mountain snowmelt, but instead their Mother River, the
great Missouri, the lifeblood of the land, was swelling like
the bloated carcass of a buffalo that had been swept away
by the long-ago river. The lapping waters slowly swallowed
the whole world they had known.

The completion of the Garrison Dam across the Missouri in 1956 was nearly a fatal blow to the traditional
culture of Louis Two Ravens' people, the Mandan,
Hidatsa, and Arickara tribes of the Fort Berthold Reservation in North Dakota. A postwar pork barrel project of
the western politicians, the dam was bitterly opposed by
the Three Tribes. After years of pressure and dirty tricks

1

from Washington and the glowing promise of the benefits to be had from a recreational lake, not to mention the "just compensation" that would never materialize, the tribal council finally relented. An old photograph of the forced signing-away of their land shows the white politicians looking well pleased while the tribal chairman weeps bitterly over the loss of his people's river. It was only the latest in a long series of tragedies that ensued almost from their first meetings with the white man. Yet somehow Louis's people survived, as they had for generations beyond count in the harsh environment of the northern plains.

Louis Two Ravens Irwin claimed blood from all three tribes. His Mandan, Hidatsa, and Arickara peoples had been living on the Great Plains for many generations before the Sioux, Cheyenne, and other tribes that are usually associated with the plains had been driven westward by eastern tribes well armed with the white man's guns. The Three Tribes survived remarkably well and maintained a rich material and ceremonial culture in the harsh northern plains because the river provided well for them. They called the river "Grandmother," and their fortified earth lodge villages clung to her banks. Along the bottoms they planted their large fields of corn and other crops that they had adapted over many generations to the harsh climate. At certain times they would abandon their villages to camp in tipis out on the plains and hunt their other great food source, the buffalo. But always to the river they returned, where they found timber, shelter, an abundance of berries and fish, and many other foods and medicines.

The Three Tribes had long been an important hub of ancient trade routes, and many tribes found their way to the Missouri to trade for the earth lodge villagers' corn and their beautifully worked skins and other crafts. To the nomadic newcomers to the Great Plains the villagers also taught plains survival skills and rituals for the buffalo. The newcomers observed such ceremonies as the Okeepa of the Mandan, which is recognized by many tribes as the "mother" of the Sun Dance.

The nomadic tribes that came to trade also came to raid and pillage when they could, and though they were a generous and peaceable people, the earth lodge dwellers maintained a strong warrior tradition and warrior societies to defend their villages. Their chiefs and leaders were those that had not only proven their bravery but also had shown respect and consideration for the elderly, the young, the weak. Their chiefs were reputed to be generous to a fault, and early white visitors remarked on how the chiefs were some of the poorest in the tribe, for they gave away whatever was needed by their people.

The land was filled with spirits: some that were ambivalent toward the people, but many that could lend their powers and aid to those they pitied and favored, those that fasted and sacrificed and prayed to the Creator and lived in a good way. There are still sacred bundles kept among Louis's people that commemorate a power that was given by the spirits through the vision of one of their own who had sacrificed to bring something of worth to the tribe. Through the sacred bundles the people could call on those powers to aid in their lives and in their survival. There were bundles and ceremonies to bring the rain, to protect their crops of corn and beans and squash, and to call the buffalo. For many years the sacred bundles were kept hidden and ceremonies were conducted in secret, for the government had outlawed any practice of their spiritual ways.

Their bundles were not just ancient relics, and some were added to or created as the spirits commanded through the visions received by the people. Today more and more people are going out to the hills to fast and pray, and the visions are returning.

Some of the Mandan people tell how Lone Man and First Creator made the land. Lone Man shaped the lands north of the Missouri. They say that Jesus was born on the other side of the world, but on this continent they had Lone Man. At times he would come to them or be born into the tribe and teach them many things. He would also come when the People were in great difficulty. When the Great Flood came, Lone Man made an enclosure for them to survive. He had said that the flood would come only to the first outer ring of the enclosure and no further, and the People would survive, and that is what happened. Forever after, the Mandan kept a shrine in the center of the village: a cedar tree, which stood for the body of Lone Man, within a circular wooden enclosure, which represented the "corral" in which Lone Man had saved them. On another level of symbolism there also stood the Tree of Life within the Sacred Hoop. Now, it may be that within the Sacred Hoop the Three Tribes will survive as a people even after they lost nearly everything and were forced to flee to the barren hills to escape the damming of the Grandmother River and the flooding of their homes.

When Lone Man left them for the last time he went to the south but promised one day to return. There are other prophecies: that one day the lake would return to a river; that a white-skinned people that they had met early in their migrations, a people they had lived with and shared with, would also return from the south, from the direction in which they had wandered off long ago.

There were few tribes that were as generous and willing to work out peace as the Mandan, Hidatsa, and Arickara. Though they had welcomed the white man and remained ever after at peace with him, few tribes had suffered a more relentless destruction of life and culture.

Just as the earth lodge people's generosity and supplies of corn drew the nomadic tribes, so were the white men drawn to their villages. Lewis and Clark wintered in a village of the Mandan. The traders that later pushed up the Grandmother River took advantage of the villagers' ancient calling as generous hosts and willing traders, and the villages became centers for the fur trade. Famous artists such as George Catlin and Karl Bodmer captured some of their rich and vibrant culture on canvas. The advantages to Louis's people were short-lived, though, for in the close quarters of the villages the white man's diseases caused devastating epidemics. In 1837 a steamboat brought smallpox to the Mandan; in a matter of months four-fifths of their people died, and the Hidatsa were reduced to half their number. Cholera, whooping cough, and measles all took their toll, until finally the survivors of the Mandan and Hidatsa, who had long been closely allied and spoke related Siouan languages, joined forces with the Arickara, who were a Caddoan people more closely related to the Pawnee. Initially they joined together for mutual defense against the nomadic tribes that preyed on them in their weakness.

At a bend in the Missouri they called Like-a-Fish-Hook, the three tribes of earth lodge people built a village. Here they attempted to resurrect their clans and ceremonies and began a closer sharing of cultural ways. Here they planted their extensive gardens and tried to start anew. The white men were not satisfied, though, and it became Indian policy to finish their job of cultural genocide by assimilating the native peoples into white culture and cultural values. One of the biggest obstacles, they thought, to "civilizing" them was the natives' practice of communal living and ownership. In order to do away with their communal ways, the government passed the Dawes Act in 1887, and as took place on every other reservation, the people of Like-a-Fish-Hook village were forced to accept allotments of 160 acres. When the last ones left the village, the Indian agent had their earth lodges torn down so that they would never return.

Louis's people set out to settle on farmsteads and built the white man's square cabins. Some of the elders would say that the People lost their power when they traded their ancient round earth lodges, which were symbolic of the universe itself, for the white man's square houses. But the People settled in far-flung communities along their Grandmother River, according to tribal and clan affiliations, and once again did their best to preserve their cultural and spiritual ways.

Yet the government and missionaries would not be satisfied until every last vestige of their culture was destroyed. Laws were passed in Congress forbidding the practice of any of their ancient ceremonies, and the missionaries and agents were more than willing to carry them out. There were fines and withholding of rations for those that were caught conducting any kind of ceremony, or for doctoring in their old ways; for a second offense they were thrown into jail. The ceremonies thus had to be performed with much secrecy. Even the ancient ceremony blessing their corn seed was forbidden. Children were taken from their homes and enrolled in the mission schools, where they were beaten for speaking their own language and forced to pray to the white man's god. Those that accepted Christianity were rewarded with favoritism.

Many of Louis's people had come far down the white man's road, and many embraced his religion. With the white man's tools they continued to plant large gardens in the Missouri bottoms. They planted grain, raised cattle, hunted and fished, and lived out to a great degree the white man's goals of turning the Indians into self-sufficient farmers. Of course, Louis's people had always been farmers, and they fared much better than those starving tribes to whom farming was foreign and who were forced onto land ill suited for any kind of agriculture.

Once more the Three Tribes had used the same fortitude and the same genius they had for adapting to the harsh northern plains to take the best of the white man's ways and use them to remain a people. But even as they were adapting to new ways, the government and white ranchers had been carving out huge tracts of their extensive lands, guaranteed to them as a nation by the solemn word of the United States in the Fort Laramie Treaty in 1868. Much land was sold off to white people after the Dawes Act. Most was simply taken without compensation, or with promises that never materialized.

Finally the government dealt them an almost fatal act of cultural genocide; they dammed their river and flooded their homes. There was no more center, for the river had always provided for them and was the foundation of their lives and their spiritual ways. Close-knit communities and clans were scattered and separated by the waters of Lake Sakakawea. Alcoholism, broken families, and despair, things that had been almost foreign to the Three Tribes, became all too commonplace. Louis Two Ravens Irwin had been born into two very different worlds, and now one of them was suddenly shattered.

# 1

# OLD DAYS AT NISHU

So many things have changed at my home. I was born into the Prairie Chicken clan in 1933 at Elbowoods, a little community by the Missouri River on the Fort Berthold Reservation that is now under the waters of a man-made lake. My father, Louis Irwin Sr., was three-quarters Mandan and one-quarter Hidatsa; his Indian name was Two Men. My mother, Clara Cora Hopkins, was three-quarters Arickara and one-quarter Hidatsa. Soon after I was born my grandfather gave me the nickname "Funny" because I was born with reddish hair and light eyes. My father had hazel eyes. Ever since the white men first came, they had noticed that many of the Mandan had light skin and eyes, and they had all kinds of theories that we were the Lost Tribes of Israel or had married with the Vikings. That name Funny stuck with me because I was always joking around. I had also been given the name Four Bears. The most famous Mandan leader of the last century was named Four Bears, and because many landmarks at Fort Berthold commemorate the famous Four Bears, I always felt too humble to use that name. Our family name on my father's side was Flies Away. My grandfather was given his "school name," Joseph Irwin, at boarding school. He used to say that he didn't mind Irwin too much because it sounds like it has "wind" in it and kind of relates to Flies Away. Besides me there was my older brother, Dreke, my younger brother, Kenny, and my sister, Donna. I also had a beautiful little sister, Frances, who died of a brain tumor when she was young.

In those days my people's communities and farms were all up and down the bottoms of the river, and a beautiful road with big trees all along it connected the communities. Today, places that were just down the river might be a two-hour drive around the lake.

My mother and father worked hard, sometimes picking beans and other jobs for white farmers, moving frequently, trying to get ahead. A lot of my early raising was with our many relations, and this was a happy time for me. It seemed like wherever I was, I was at home and everyone was my relation. Wherever I wound up at night I would sleep, I would be fed and taken care of, and my parents never worried. I had a grandmother that took care of me, Ella Waters, my Arickara grandpa's second wife. Many people remember her as a medicine woman. I can remember being very small and while I lay there she would touch my ears and eyes and fingers and say, "Oh, look at these: they are so beautiful, they are miracles; these are gifts from the Creator. These eyes; with these eyes you can see the Creator's miracles. These ears can here the drum. You must take care of these gifts. How could anyone ever harm them?"

My people had always been farmers, and I remember the big community gardens where we grew corn, squash, beans, potatoes, turnips, melons, and just about anything else you can think of. We kids helped in the gardens, but we did a lot of running around and playing too. I remember the grown-ups used to turn bull snakes loose in the gardens to eat the rodents and chase the rattlesnakes away;

even though they were harmless, it'd scare the heck out of you when you'd come up on one.

My people were self-sufficient; all we had to trade for was some salt and coffee and flour. North Dakota is a cold place, but the people had lots of timber and firewood that grew along the river bottoms. Many families even had little mines of coal that they would dig by hand out of the hillsides in the Badlands. We hunted deer, rabbits, and prairie chickens and ate fish from the river. Along the Missouri we gathered bushels of plums and chokecherries and bullberries. My people were also successful ranchers and had big herds of horses and cattle, our new buffalo.

We called the Missouri the "Grandmother River." The river was clear in those days, and we'd get barrels of water from the river and let it settle. That was our drinking water. I remember that when the men would be returning from riding off in the Badlands, the horses would smell the water first and pick up their heads. Then the men would say, "We're almost home!"

There was very little alcohol around when I was growing up. There were just a few drunks; the people made fun of them, but they were still taken care of. Many of my people were already Christians then, and many were going the white man's way of making money, but the People seemed to get along. We were taught to treat each one as a relative. Anytime there was a feast or a ceremony or a gathering, at the end everyone, young and old, would stand in a line and shake hands. Even if you had just seen someone yesterday, you would shake that person's hand.

Many times I would stay with my mother's father at Nishu, an Arickara community now also under the waters of the lake. My parents wanted me to stay with my grandfather not just because they had to work a lot but also for my education. My grandfather's name was George Hopkins. His Indian name was Red Star. He was a holy man among his Arickara people. Grandpa farmed grain and had cattle—I remember the tall Stetson hat he always wore—but he was also very traditional. My grandfather's ways opened a whole new world for me.

There were always kids around my grandpa, and he was always teaching us, getting us to watch, to listen to nature and the world around us. Grandpa would take us out into the Badlands and show us fossils and the layers of rock. He would tell us about the many ages when these rocks had been laid down, when these ancient animals had lived. He told us that the rocks had seen many things through the centuries while they watched the stars and the sun and the moon. The rocks had many things to teach us about the ancient history of the Earth Mother.

Grandpa taught us about the ways and habits of the animals. He would say, "We were the last to be created. The animals are our elder relations and have much wisdom to teach. They walk the way of the Earth and the ways they were given by the Creator. Whoever walks the way of the Earth walks a good road."

And Grandpa always taught us to walk carefully, to be aware of every little thing. One day we were walking along by the creek that ran behind my grandpa's place. There was an old, brown, dried-up log in the path that I always had to climb over.

"How many times have you climbed right over this log?" Grandpa asked. "Let me show you something. There is a whole world right here."

Grandpa lifted up the log and told me to get down and look closely. I got down on my knees and peered under the log. Grandpa was right: there was a whole world under there. Bugs were running around in all directions. Some of them were scurrying around gathering up food. Others seemed to be trying to save their little home.

Grandpa put the log back carefully and told me, "Just as we are looking at their world, there is someone who is looking down on us. This is their little world. They go out from their village to hunt and gather food, and they bring it home to their people. We have no reason to disturb their world. Someone could come along and take this log, and maybe if they're careful and don't disturb things too much, these bugs can find another log or someplace to live. If you were starving you might have to eat some of them, but there's no reason to destroy the whole village.

"Whenever we see living things we must respect their right to live. They are our relatives. We disturb them or eat them only when we have to, to survive. Whenever we do that we leave a space, a hole in the Creator's world. Go to your uncles and see what they do. When they kill a deer, they put tobacco there and talk to their brother. When they release the spirit, they put down tobacco to help in a humble way to cover that hole they made in the world. They ask the Creator to accept their small offering and prayer, for it is the best we can do as pitiful human beings."

Grandpa's house was big, but it always seemed warm to me, even when it was very cold out. There were a lot of talks around the big wood cookstove where Grandma kept the coffee on and made good things to eat. One of my clearest memories was of staring at the big gourd rattles that were hanging over Grandpa's bed. He used them in doctoring and in the ceremonies. After I stood there a while I thought I could hear them going *tchk, tchk, tchk.*

I remember certain things about my people's ceremonies and ways of worship, but many things I was too young to understand. Many of those things are lost now. The Arickaras had a big roundhouse where they held their ceremonies. It had two doors, to the east and west. I remember a corn dance, as well as a bear dance and other dances where it seemed like the men actually became the animals. They dressed in skins and made noises and acted just like the animals. I can remember the bears lunging at the people who were roped off from the dancers and getting scared. The Arickaras were known for their healing ceremonies, where they would perform all different kinds of magical acts; at one ceremony they carried in a woman on a platform to be healed. I can remember the Mandan and Hidatsa women's Goose Dance, a ceremony for the Old Woman Who Never Dies. She is a spirit of my people who, they say, calls the birds and other animals back in the spring. The geese are her messengers, and the deer tend her gardens. The people appealed to her for good crops and good weather.

There were Sun Dances in those days, put on by the Hidatsa. They were always held way out in the Badlands. I didn't know it then, but the government had outlawed the Sun Dance as a barbaric ceremony back in the 1890s. I remember there being only a few out there dancing; these few danced as a sacrifice for all the People. There weren't a hundred or more people dancing as there are at some Sun Dances today.

The Sun Dance of the northern plains actually came from my people through our ancient ceremonies such as the Okeepa ceremony of the Mandans and the Hide-Beating ceremony of the Hidatsa. In the Okeepa there were a few men who gave of their flesh or hung from the poles in sacrifice for the People. In the Okeepa ceremony they also brought into the circle painted dancers that represented the moon and stars and day and night, as well as animals that represented the Creation. At my home there are people who have had the visions to revive this ancient ceremony.

I can remember ceremonies with the Sacred Pipe, our most sacred instrument of worship. Through the pipe we pray to our Creator. I remember the people's houses: there would always be gourd rattles and sacred bundles hanging in the bedrooms, and I can still see the way they looked in the light of the kerosene lamps. They would spread blankets on the floor, and the people, elders and little children, all would sit together and smoke the Sacred Pipe. It made us kids feel happy to be accepted into the grownups' circle that way.

As far back as I can remember I've been raised with

the sweat lodge, the sacred Lodge of Purification, though it was only much later that I understood some of the many symbols and meanings of the ceremony. I can remember sticking my head out of the covers of the lodge, while my cousin always cried. For a long time I thought none of the elders knew about me sticking out my head, but when I grew a little older they used to tease me about it. Those sweats seemed like they were always joyful. There wasn't as much ceremony involved with the Arickaras' Purification Lodge as with the Mandans' or the Lakotas'. The people would call on the spirits and pray that everyone should eat well and feel good, and that the world would be good. Those were the kind of prayers I remember.

The sweat lodge is more properly called the Lodge of Purification. We don't go in there just to sweat, like in a sauna. This is where we go to purify not just our bodies but also the mind and the spirit. Before any important ceremony or undertaking we go into the Purification Lodge. Everything connected with it is full of meaning. It is our church. It's not fancy; we don't build a big building to impress the Creator, just some bent willows. But those willows stand for something. They stand for the strength of the willow, and the green things that grow from the earth. All the elements of creation are there: the earth, the fire, the water, and the air. We show respect to the grandfather rocks that we use, for they are the oldest; they are a part of the original creation. When we crawl into the Purification Lodge, we are crawling into the Earth Mother's womb. We go in there to be reborn. In the darkness of the womb we sing the songs that call for the spirits to join us. We pray for all living things. We try to leave our bad thoughts and sicknesses in there; we give them to the rocks. We pour the water of life on the grandfather rocks that have been heated in the sacred fire, and the breath of the grandfathers purifies us and strengthens our spirit.

The Purification Lodge is very ancient, and not just

among my people. The sweat lodge was used in Europe thousands of years ago. When I was young I would see my people go off into the Badlands by some stream or by the Missouri far away from anyone and set up sweat lodges, where they would sweat and have ceremony for five or six days. I wondered why we didn't do this at our homes; we had creeks and water there, too. The Sun Dances were always held way out in the Badlands, and sentinels on the hills around would watch for any intruders. People performing ceremonies in their houses would always cover the windows before they started.

So one day I asked my grandfather, "Why do we always go far off to have our sweats? Why are the Sun Dances so secret? Why do we cover the windows up when we have ceremonies?"

And so it was that my grandfather sat me down and told me of the American, the Invader. How the white people came here for religious freedom and denied it to the people that were already here. They showed us how they preach love for their god, who was supposed to be a god of love, and showed us that love by kidnapping us away and beating us in their schools, by shaving our heads. The more Grandpa spoke about it, the more I could see what they had done to us. But I could not understand how people could do that to another people.

I told my grandfather how that hurt me. He said that he felt bad about it too, but that the vision said we will one day return. This vision said that a people will try to get into the circle with us, and that we must bring them in. In that time the very religion and way of worship that they are trying to destroy will be the very way of worship and the instruments of worship that will be the salvation for the Mother Earth. I believed this and I believe it now.

My grandfather held me as he told me that no matter what, I should never bow down to anyone except the Creator, the Grandfather, God.

# 2

# MISSION SCHOOL

My grandfather was always teaching me. I didn't know it then, but what he was teaching was the Old Ways, ways that many in my parents' generation were trying to leave behind. My father and mother had both been sent to boarding schools, where they were taught to look down on the ways of our ancestors. My father still had a lot of respect for the Old Ways, but he was busy trying to make it in the white man's world.

Grandpa and I used to spend a lot of time fishing. We used to fish with lines, and Grandpa also had fish traps that were made in the old way out of woven willows. There was even a ceremony that went along with the traps; Grandpa said he had "captured" that ceremony from the Hidatsas.

One day we were cleaning a bunch of bullheads down in the little creek by his place. There is a little white air sac in the fish; I think it helps them to float. Grandpa always told me that if I ate that sac it would make me a good, strong swimmer. My mother had come down there while I was washing one of those sacs and saw me pop it into my mouth.

"What are you doing," she said, "eating those things? You didn't even cook it!" She was upset, even though I tried to explain what Grandpa had told me.

Later on Grandpa called me over and said, "You've got to take care of your body, Grandson. That fish, he lives strong in that water, and when you take him into you, his strength goes into you. Your mother doesn't know these things."

These were the Old Ways I was learning. But many of the things I learned were about how a person is supposed to live. And Grandpa always tried to make a lesson in the things we did. He would say, "All these things that happen to you—if you don't learn, it's for nothing! Remember how you didn't cinch your saddle tight and you fell off your horse? The next time you forget to cinch it tight you could be off somewhere and your horse will throw you; you could break a leg and you'd never make it home. Try to learn as you go along.

"It's like the 'throwing the hoop' game. They're rolling the hoop and you're all trying to hit it with your arrow. Maybe one of the boys throwing an arrow is taller and stronger than you, but if you watch the person instead of the hoop you'll never hit the hoop. You watch the hoop and you learn to judge so maybe you have to throw your arrow a little harder and ahead of the hoop next time. As you go along you must try to learn."

Grandpa told little stories, usually about animals or people who did foolish things, and there was always a lesson in them. One was the story of the heron and the frogs. The frogs had a great chief that passed on, and they wanted to find a new leader. Some frogs were wise and good, but the group decided they wanted a leader who was more grand and powerful. They looked to the other animals, trying to decide who would be a powerful and majestic chief for the frogs. They saw the great heron, standing so proud and tall and beautiful, and the frogs asked him, "O

Great Heron, you stand so tall and powerful. Would you be our great and mighty chief?" The great heron agreed to be their chief, and then he ate up every one of those frogs!

My grandfather didn't always teach me with words and stories. Sometimes I would be sitting out on a big rock by the creek, just thinking about things, and he would come and sit by me and not say anything. Even when he did speak, he never spoke down to me; he spoke to me like I was already one of the grown men. That made me feel humble, because you could see how the People respected him when they came around. He not only doctored and led ceremonies but was also a counselor for the People. I remember how they would bring little gifts to him and Grandpa would go off and sit and talk with them. So we'd be sitting on that rock, and maybe I'd be troubled about something, but he wouldn't say anything or ask me to say anything. We'd just sit there. After a long time he'd grab my knee and say, "Come on, Grandson, let's go get some coffee," and we'd eat pan bread and drink coffee and talk.

But the white government had other plans for Indian kids, and they didn't include learning traditional ways and living close to the Earth. Once they had figured out we weren't going to disappear, they decided that they could take us away as children and try to force us to become like white people.

One day when I was still very young, I was back home with my parents, and the Indian police came to take me away to mission school. My mother was crying pitifully, and I felt very bad. I had never ridden on a bus before, and a bunch of other Indian kids were all crowded on there. We were given bologna and an apple. I had never had bologna either.

Even now I can remember the pain and the fear and the humiliation I felt when we arrived at the school. We were stripped naked and sprayed for lice, and our heads were shaved. It makes me cry to think of my little friends standing there naked. Some of the other kids were so scared that they peed on themselves. We learned to fear what they called the "beaver tail," a big leather strap with holes in it, with so many hits for such-and-such offense: so many for singing Indian songs, so many for talking your language, so many for acting Indian. It makes me cry to think of little children being pushed around and whipped and beaten by someone so much bigger than them. They made us eat their strange food, and they made us eat it all; if we threw up in our bowls, they made us eat that too. This was my introduction to the white world.

I was always getting into trouble. One time I had found crayons that were of the sacred colors we use in our ceremonies. I melted them on the radiator to make paint for my face. I got in a lot of trouble for that one. My grandpa had given me a special rock from our home. They took it away from me; they said I was going to hit someone with it.

I would try to burn a little sage, and if I couldn't get sage I would burn some weeds and pray to the Grandfather that he would accept such pitiful smoke offerings. I liked the way the smoke smelled; it reminded me of my home and of our sacred ceremonies. One time I was caught by the janitor, and he accused me of trying to start a fire; he really threw me around.

A group of boys formed our own club. We would meet behind the barn where they kept the cows and chickens. One boy was the lookout. We had one rule there: no English could be spoken! We had our little round Quaker Oats boxes that they gave us to put our comb and brush and things in; we used those for our drums. We would dance and sing our people's songs: ceremonial songs, sweat lodge songs, social songs. We would learn each other's songs. It's a good thing they never caught us.

Of course, they also tried to teach us the white man's religion. When I look back now I know they taught us all the negative, scary parts of their religion; all about sin and hell and punishment. I was afraid of the white man's God and always thought he was really going to give it to me. We were told that if we were good and followed this way that when we got to heaven we would become white people. I thought that was the scariest part of all!

I had made it to the fifth grade in boarding school. One day I was shooting marbles down on the ground with my friends when I saw some men walking toward us. I could see by the Stetson hat that it was Grandpa. He was with two of my uncles, and a white man was walking beside them, excited and angry. Grandpa pulled me up to my feet and told me to come with him, I was leaving this place. I told him I needed to get my clothes and things, but he said, "That's OK. Forget those things. Let's go." And he took me out of school just like that.

A few months later a white woman and the Indian police came to our home to take me back to school, and I can remember my mother crying pitifully again. I didn't last long, though; the night after I got back to school I tied some sheets together and slipped out the dormitory window. I ran to where they were having a big powwow not far away. We used to call them "doings." I danced all night and never went back to school until many years later.

Today I pray and I cry in the sweat lodge, and I thank the ancestors who suffered so we could have a spiritual way of life. I thank them for their sacrifices so I may go into the sweat lodge and into the sacred Sun Dance circle and smoke the Sacred Pipe. Many white people and even many young Indians do not know of the sacrifices made and how hard the government and missionaries tried to stamp out our way of life. Sometimes I wonder about those people that beat us, and I wonder how they were greeted by the Great Spirit. I didn't feel hatred then, though later I did; but I felt wonder and confusion at how someone big could raise a hand against someone so small, and I wonder if they went home at night and loved their own children. I wonder if they can see us now that we have children of our own and are practicing our way of life.

The white man's schools did much to contribute to the alcoholism and broken families and despair that plague my people. My own father was sent away to boarding school, and the practice goes back to the last century. What does it do to a person's self-esteem to be taught that his culture was worthless, to be beaten for speaking his language? What kind of parent can you learn to be if you are taken from all the ones you love and punished instead of loved? You have people that don't know how to hug their own children, or even worse, have been taught that violence should be used against children. This was not our way. In our Old Ways a child was given love and affection by a large extended family, and a child was never beaten.

Now when I go into the museums I can see what the government and invaders tried to do: they tried to wipe us out. And when they couldn't kill us all, they tried to make us forget and placed our culture behind a glass case. It's as if we were already extinct. I feel as if our whole world was a little earth under my fingernail. They could take all our instruments of worship and punish us in their schools and everything else, but as long as we have that bit of earth, we will remain a people.

The Indian people have never tried to force their ways on anyone. Now there are many that come to us hungry to learn. When they come we will not beat them and make them pee on themselves, or pinch their backs, or sling them to the ground, or cut their hair. Instead, for those that come in a good way and are ready to listen, we will bring them into the sacred Lodge of Purification and say, "Welcome home."

# 3

# Into the Badlands

When I was little my grandfather would tell me about certain things I needed to learn for the time when he would take me off into the Badlands and I would have to survive on my own for a while. After I quit school he began to prepare me, showing me how to set snares for rabbits, how to build a little shelter, how to catch fish without a hook, and how to identify the roots and things I could eat to survive.

I was only twelve years old when my grandfather told me it was time to go; he said I was going to be alone for seven days in the Badlands. I may have been the last of my generation to be sent out in this ancient way. This vigil in the wilderness was not a test of manhood or necessarily for "seeking a vision," as the books call it. The purpose was to know the world of the parents we are all born to, the Mother Earth and the Father Sky, to know how much we are dependent on them, and to know that we are never truly alone in this world.

My grandpa and I drove a long way toward the Little Missouri Badlands. We came to a place where many of my relations and people were gathered; I wasn't to speak, though. A sweat lodge was prepared, and after I was purified I came out of the lodge and saw two horses waiting, all saddled up. Grandpa and I rode west along the bottoms into the Badlands.

As we rode along Grandpa gave me instructions on how to conduct myself humbly before the Earth and the spirits, and he reminded me to be watchful for the teachings and lessons I would learn. I was given a knife, a .22 rifle and eight bullets, some leather and some green rawhide string, and a little food. I also carried some prayer ties, cloth and tobacco offerings that were made by my relations as they prayed for me.

Finally we stopped at a canyon where the Little Missouri flows out of the Badlands. "This is where I will leave you. Walk until night comes, and walk tomorrow until the sun is straight overhead. That's where you will make your camp." Grandpa made a prayer to the Great Spirit and to the Earth and her creatures to protect and watch over me. He looked me in the eyes and spoke the last words I would hear for a week: "Remember, everything you see was created by the Great Spirit and has something to teach. Everything you can see is your relative."

I watched for a long time as Grandpa disappeared, leading the horse I had ridden. I was never so alone or so far from the people who cared for me. When night came I lay down, but I don't think I got any sleep. The next day I was walking before the sun peeked over the canyon wall. When the sun was straight overhead I found myself in a beautiful valley. I found a nice bench of land between the creek and the bluffs above. This was to be home for the next seven days.

The first thing I was to do was to put up a tall staff, to which I tied my prayer offerings. The staff was to call the spirits to watch over and teach me, and also to help me find my way home. Seeing the prayer ties hanging there made me feel good because they had been made by my relatives while they prayed for me.

It was the time when the chokecherries were ripe and life was everywhere around me. Animals and snakes and bugs, everything was busy being alive. All this life made me lonelier, in a way, because I felt like I was an intruder in someone else's home. As I walked by, the birds would fly out of the trees. When I went down by the creek, the beavers would slap their tails loudly and swim away. I felt like a stranger in their world. At night all my fears would come to me. I could hear animals rustling in the brush below me; the owls and coyotes called back and forth. I thought about rattlesnakes crawling out on the warm rocks. I couldn't help thinking of the ghost stories my people tell.

I stayed busy, though, and after a few days I began to make out OK. At sunrise I would pray and do the simple ceremonies I had been taught. Before we left, Grandpa had showed me how to set up a stick in the sun and draw a circle around it with a rawhide string. Around the circle I marked the Four Directions and the divisions of the day. I began to truly see the paths of the sun and the moon as they circled over the world; I saw the circles that marked the time that is given to us. I began to see the circles of life that made each little life a part of one great circle.

I didn't go hungry, even though I missed our home cooking. I set up an old-time fish trap with stakes driven in the bottom of the creek. I set snares for rabbits and roasted them on sticks. I carefully skinned them and staked out their little hides, but they didn't cure well, as I had somehow lost the salt I had brought along. It was the time when fruits were ripening, and I had all the chokecherries, bullberries, and wild plums I could eat. I dug wild prairie turnips to eat raw or cooked in a soup; I made soup the old-time way, heating up the rocks and putting them in a skin to boil water.

I had many adventures and experienced many things that still come back to me many years later. I remember the painted cliffs above my wilderness home and the pictures and messages I saw in them. Once I found an old tomahawk and set it in a place where I might come back for it some day, with permission from my elders and the proper ceremony, the way I was taught.

I spent a lot of time playing my own games. I painted myself and danced and sang songs and attacked lots of cavalry! I found a cave and would throw things in the opening; I was curious but never could make myself crawl in there. Sometimes I would go to the top of the ridge and watch the life below me. At night I would watch the sky fill with thousands of stars. Sometimes the stars seemed close, like friends and relations; other times they seemed strange and far away.

As time passed I noticed that the animals were less and less afraid of me. They would stay near, and I could even talk to them. The ground squirrels moved into my camp and made themselves right at home, the birds no longer flew away, and even the beavers weren't slapping their tails and swimming away. The turtles and lizards and many little creatures became my new friends and relations, and I really began to feel at home.

I began to get over my fear of the darkness. I remembered how my grandpa had told me that there is nothing more to fear in the nighttime than in the day, that the spirits around us can see that much better in the day. "But for you," he said, "the darkness can be like a blanket. You can cover yourself with that blanket and feel safe. In that darkness you can see, too, and not just with your eyes."

One night I was sitting by the creek when I heard something coming toward me. There were two deer, and I could see their eyes shining in the dark. They almost walked over me, but they never did see me. I felt what my grandfather said, that the darkness was my blanket.

I had been watching the deer and learning their trails, and I made a stand at a pretty hole of water on the creek where the deer came in the morning to drink. I thought that my grandpa would be proud if I could shoot a deer and skin it. One morning a young buck came up behind a pair of does; he stood there for a long time watching over those does. I had the .22 with me, and the buck was an easy shot. But I could see his eyes and how big and beautiful he was, and I thought about how I really had plenty of food to eat at my camp. I never did get a deer. Later I found a porcupine, and I remembered my Grandpa saying that porcupines could easily be clubbed for food if I got thrown from a horse far from home or if for some other reason I was starving. But for that reason they should be respected; they had helped our people in hard times. I remembered, too, how Grandpa had taught me how to bait them with an apple on a blanket. I'd run up and roll them up in that blanket. By the time they got out there would be plenty of porcupine quills stuck on the blanket for my grandmother to do her beautiful quillwork.

As I marked off the days it got closer and closer to the day I would be leaving the Badlands and going back to my people. It made me sad because my camp was really starting to be a home, my own little place in the middle of the Creator's world. I thought that if only there was corn soup and frybread there, I could live at my camp for a long time.

It came the day to go, though. When the sun was straight up I was to start walking east. I took down the little lean-to I had made. I fed the rest of my food to the fish; my prairie turnips I left for all the rabbits that came around. I felt sad as I said good-bye to the lizards and ground squirrels that had become my friends around the camp. I felt how life was a circle—the sun and moon circling over me, the lives of the animals. I knew I would not see the deer come down to the water again before I left, and that made me sad. I took a branch and swept my camp clean;

Grandpa had said to leave my camp as if no one had been there. I did leave the staff with the tobacco offerings standing in the rocks I had piled there; that was to be an offering for the spirits of that place. I prayed to the Four Directions and thanked them for the safety I had there and for the things I had learned.

I walked for a long time to the east. In North Dakota in the late summer it stays light very late. There wasn't much light left when I could see something off in the distance. I could make out two horses, and then a man on one of the horses. It was my grandfather, and he was leading a pretty little horse that had an eagle feather tied in its mane. We rode back in silence to where the people had gathered again; I had to remain silent until I was in the sacred sweat lodge, where I could speak and tell what I had experienced. I couldn't think of much to say, though, because I had so many feelings that I couldn't put into words.

After the sweat my father presented me with the eagle feather and that pretty little horse, which I named Kilroy. The people all greeted me and shook my hand; it felt good to be back with my people again. The eagle feather was the only one I had given to me until many years later. It always makes me sad to see people begin to sun dance with no eagle feathers, because it usually means that they haven't been honored by their people, even though they may have done brave or important things in their lives.

The time I spent in the Badlands has never left me through my life. In the times of my worst fears or when I felt the most lonely or out of balance, inside I remembered that I was really at home wherever I was in this world, and over time I came to truly understand that we are all relations, we are all the children of one Father and one Mother. From our Father we have protection, and from our Mother we are given everything we need to live. Wherever we go, we are never out of their sight. I also knew that within myself, I was my own best friend.

Not long after my vigil I had a dream. I could see the staff I had left in the Badlands, and all the animals, rabbits and squirrels and deer, were carrying off my staff and the rocks I had piled up there. Before they disappeared they turned around, and they were saying, "So long. Thank you for cleaning up here. Good-bye, we'll see you!" Then I'd cry and say, "I'll be back. I'll be back." I had that dream many times. It would make me sad, but I also knew that I always had a place there, and that place was a part of me.

After my vigil in the Badlands I began to notice the things around me. It seemed that everything was speaking to me, and I could understand with my heart. I could lie down and watch the clouds change into pictures that seemed full of meaning. I watched the animals; they seemed to know me and they showed me things. When the thunder spoke, I felt it was a powerful voice calling to me.

One day I went to lie under the trees that grew in the Missouri bottoms. In those days there was a beautiful forest that grew along the river, with huge trees. Maybe I was troubled about something, and that is why I went to lie down there to think about things. I remember getting up and putting my arms around a big tree. I felt the spirit of the tree, and it made me feel good. There was something that troubled me, though, and I felt a great sadness too. Something made me worry for the trees and for the land; I felt that something was going to happen.

When I got back to my grandpa's I told him what I had felt, and he asked, "What do you think is going to happen?" I told him I didn't know, but I felt a great sadness in the trees and the land.

Sometime after that I began to hear the people speaking of what the white man was going to do. The government wanted to build a dam that would flood our beautiful valley, our homes, our timber. It seemed impossible at the time.

Even before the dam was started, my father left Fort Berthold and never returned. He told me that the dam would be the end of our people, for they had been pressured into signing away their land and their livelihood. He would have no more land, no more horses. When I was a young teenager my father moved our family to Glasgow, Montana, to get work on another dam the government was building. He hoped to save money to buy some cattle and a piece of land somewhere.

Although the Fort Peck Indian reservation was nearby, Glasgow had only five Indian families, and there was a lot of prejudice. The whole time I was growing up I saw white men once in a while, but in my world everyone was Arickaras and Mandans and Hidatsas. My first introduction to the white man's world was in mission school, where we were beaten for acting Indian. My next was in the town of Glasgow.

I do not like to speak of the things I experienced there; growing up is hard for many children, and I would rather put the feelings of anger behind me. There was the time my dad gave me money for my first ice-cream cone, and a white man came up and smashed it in my face. My father bought me a new shirt that I was really proud of; some white kids jumped me and tore off the shirt. One time I was just walking along the railroad tracks when a big white man came up behind me and kicked me in the tailbone so hard I couldn't sit down for days after. But Glasgow is also where I learned to fight and defend myself.

I was a teenager now and going through a lot of turmoil. Meanwhile, my parents had their own troubles. My mother left and never came back.

One day I was back visiting my grandfather and my uncles when they confronted me with two big decisions. One was about Kilroy, the horse they had given me. He was still wild, and they were wondering when I was going to break him. I went out with my uncles, riding Kilroy and snubbed between their horses. My legs were hitting hard against those horses. I was trying hard to stay on, but I got thrown off. Even though I was angry, at the same time I was afraid of that horse. I loved him, but he only added to my frustrations. It turned out that nobody was ever able to break Kilroy, and he became a bronc in the rodeos.

The other big decision was whether I should go off to school somewhere. I had never lasted long in a school, and I hadn't learned to read or write. It seemed that in Glasgow all I could do was get into fights and trouble. In town I had seen posters for the army, and I talked to my grandpa about it. I said, "Maybe I could go into the army, and then I could do something. They teach you things in there." I was only fifteen then, and I knew I'd have to wait a few years to go. All I knew was that I had to do something.

I was sitting out on a big rock in the creek behind my grandfather's place. When I saw it again years later I realized it wasn't really such a big rock. But it was important to me, the place where I used to go to sit and think. And just as he used to, Grandpa came and sat down beside me without saying anything. Pretty soon he put his hand on my knee and said, "Come on, Grandson, let's go get some coffee."

It was in the evening. We were eating pan bread and drinking coffee. After a while my grandfather said, "There's always something in your mind you can't do. Should you break that horse? Should you go off far away? Should you do this, should you do that? You never go and talk to the spirits anymore. Tomorrow we'll get up early in the morning. We'll have a sweat and we'll go off on horseback, then I'll leave you and come back for you in the evening."

It wasn't even daylight yet when we went out. My two uncles had the fire going, and the rocks were ready. While we had our sweat my grandfather told me that if I got lost I should wait until the early morning, then look for the Little Dipper and the morning star to find my way home. "Or," he said, "you can look at that person that walks behind you and he can tell you how to go home." That was so I could get scared and say, "Well, I'm not going then."

That got me worried, and I can remember getting out of the sweat lodge and asking my grandfather, "What about that person that walks behind me? Who is that?"

"I don't know," he said. "It's a ghost or something. Now you have another decision. Are you going to go out there? Are you scared? Are you going to go off? Are you going to break that horse? Go and talk."

So we rode off toward the Badlands. Grandpa and my uncles left me there and took off. I had a little frybread and some dried meat. I sat a while and tried to pray, but I didn't really know what I was praying about. Mostly I just walked around.

Everything was interesting to me back then—different rocks, insects, and all sorts of things. I came across an anthill, a pretty big one. The ants were big too, and they were running around all over the place. I watched them closely and saw that they were carrying something white back into the hole. It looked like bread, but I knew it couldn't be bread way out here. The pieces were three times bigger than they were, but they were running with it and carrying pieces down that hole.

One ant had a really big piece of whatever it was, and it wouldn't fit in the hole. He tried and tried, and the other ants would run on top of him; it looked like they were biting him and kicking him. He held on to it, but he couldn't get it down that hole. I got a little stick and was going to get up and help him, but just about that time the ant somehow shifted that piece of something around and got it down the hole. I walked around more, but no prayers or lessons seemed to come to me.

Late in the evening my uncles came. They didn't say anything as we rode back. It was dark when we returned, and we had a joyful sweat. I call it that because that's how I remember it; a lot of laughter and joy, and not too hot. Not like when it was cold out or you had a cough or something; then Grandpa would make it really hot.

Grandpa waited until I was out of the sweat, then he asked me, "So, what did you see out there?"

Grandma said, "Oh, leave him alone." But they asked again what I had seen, and I told them, "Nothing."

"You went all around out there and you didn't see anything? You didn't even talk to a tree?"

"Well," I said, "I prayed to God, I guess . . . Oh, yeah! I saw these ants. They were all working and carrying big pieces of something into their house, and one couldn't get it into the hole. He kept trying and trying, and the other ones were biting him and running over him, but he never let go of what he had. I got a stick and was going to help him, but he finally got it into their house."

My grandfather turned to me and said, "The biggest thing happened. You were given a lesson. You were blessed. They poked you in the ribs, and you didn't even feel it! Now you will think about your decisions. Whatever you're going to do, you're going to do. You'll make some good decisions in your life. One day you'll be my chief and make me proud of you. You're going to do and see a lot of things. But today this ant, this little person, showed you what he can do and what you can do—even though he is much stronger than you are. If you were as strong as him, you could lift up a house and walk away with it. But that ant person went with what he had. Even his own brothers didn't help him. But he went and took what he had; whatever his goal was, he took it and brought it into the house. That's what you've got to do. Pick it up, regardless of who is going to help you. Go with it the best you can."

Grandma came up and gave me a hug, "See," she said, "they poked you. They're always poking you!"

That is a story I never shared with many people. Those are the animals that seem to come to me: the little ones, like a frog. The frog is important to me, and the ant. They may not seem like majestic Indian animals, like eagles or wolves, but I've thought of that ant many times: in Korea, when I wondered how I could ever make it out of that place alive; when I walked into a college classroom for the first time with only a fifth-grade education; and at times when I knew in my heart that something was right, but it seemed like the whole world was against me.

# 4

# TRIAL BY FEAR

Things still weren't going well for me in Glasgow, Montana. I was always fighting any kid that called me a "dirty Injun." But I started taking boxing lessons, and I discovered that I was a natural. I was able to use all that anger that was inside me to win bouts. If my opponent got the first punch in, that made me really mad, and sometimes I knocked out guys with my first punch. For a while I was the district champion boxer for my age.

The first time I got drunk I was fourteen; some friends and I got a man to buy us a case of beer. Right from the start, when I drank I would become someone else—a crazy person. I started finding other kinds of trouble to get into, and one time a friend of mine and a girl "borrowed" a car for a joyride. The cops started chasing us, and pretty soon they were shooting at us. My friend finally stopped, and he and the girl took off running. I had rolled into the ditch to keep from getting shot, but I still got hit in the leg. The sheriff walked up and started kicking me over and over.

They hauled me to jail, and finally my grandmother came and told them that if they turned me over to her she would see that I went into the army. She was my father's mother, Laura Two Crows Horn. She had a way of demanding respect. When she would go to Parshall, a town near Fort Berthold, she'd just hold her hand up to stop traffic and take her time crossing the street; that's the way she was. I had talked with my relations about joining the army when I was old enough; Now I was only seventeen years old, but my grandmother signed for me to get into the army. It was that or a juvenile home. At the time I had never heard of Korea.

I went through boot camp all right, and then we were shipped off to Korea. A lot of Indians volunteered to go to Korea, just as they had in World War II. It was a way to get away from the problems and the poverty on the reservations, a way to prove ourselves. We were told that we were the "policemen of the world," and I thought I was really going to do something good and brave to make the world a safe place. Even though Korea was a strange place, I made out OK. I found out I could keep up with guys that were a lot older than me. I was with the Eighth Ranger Company, Twenty-fifth Division; we were the guys that got sent to the front lines. They put a gun in my hand, but I was still just a kid.

At first it didn't seem like I was in the middle of a war; it was more like a Hollywood war movie. There was a routine you did every day: check your socks, clean your rifle, check your ammo. And that's how it went for me at first. Most of our fighting was shooting at long distances; we hardly ever saw the enemy face to face. You couldn't tell whose bullet killed someone.

A lot of the guys in my company were Indians of different tribes. One day there was a firefight around a little Korean village. When the firing stopped we went into the village. The huts were burning, and some of our guys were going around shooting pigs and chickens and anything that moved. In front of one hut were fourteen Korean bodies laid out in a row. A group of us Indians was standing there, and I think we all felt at the same time that these people looked a lot like us. They could have been our relations. They were more like us than the guys we were fighting for. It's still clear in my mind how one of the Navajos started emptying the tobacco out of a pack of cigarettes. He went over and placed an offering of tobacco at the head of each body. Even though we were from different tribes, we all knew what he was doing, and we began to pray and sing in our own languages. We held a ceremony right there in the middle of a war.

A soldier who was standing there watching us said, "Ah, they're doing that 'cause they look just like 'em." But later my lieutenant came over and asked me about it. He wondered how we all got together on that, and I explained that the ceremony wasn't something we planned or something we had learned; it was just something we all felt. After that he'd talk with me a lot about my people and their ways, and about what a crazy war we were in.

Things got a lot more serious after that. We were sent out on patrols into rough country. It was getting to be wintertime, and it was really cold. They assigned me a Korean arms bearer for the explosives and the big automatic weapon I carried. His name was Kim. He was quite a few years older than I was, and we got to be good friends. Kim taught me a lot about how to survive in Korea: where to find water, how to find food, where to find caves and places to hide.

The fighting got heavier and closer at hand. It suddenly hit me that I was in a real war, not a Hollywood movie, and all my fear began to come out. I thought for sure I would get shot, and I had seen guys get shot up in every way you can be wounded. Which would be worse: to lose an arm, a leg, or an eye? I didn't want to get shot in the balls, for sure. And if I died, I wanted to die in one piece so I could look good when my people honored me.

I still remember seeing the bloated bodies of the dead, stacked like firewood, rotting in the sun before they could be hauled away. I remember the smell of death; it is a smell that never leaves you.

I witnessed what they called the Tunnel Massacre. The North Koreans had a bunch of U.S. soldiers in a tunnel where they blindfolded them and shot every one of them in the head. We took over their position and they surrendered. When troops went in the tunnel and saw what they had done, they executed every one of those Koreans. I saw them do it.

In another battle I saw my arms bearer, Kim, get shot. He was carried off, and I never learned if he lived or not. I've thought about him a lot over the years. I've wondered if he lived to see the same day I was seeing, if he lived to see his family again. Sometimes he is in my dreams.

I began to know in my heart that I was fighting people who were more like my people than the government I was fighting for—the government that had invaded our land in the first place. At the same time, I became angry with the North Koreans; why couldn't they just give up so this bloody mess could be over?

It was fear that made me able to kill. I was becoming what the army trained me to be. The first time you know you have killed someone, you feel deep remorse. Then you have to do it again, and it becomes a little easier. But there is always the remorse and always the nightmares after. And each time, something inside you dies.

The fighting became worse and worse—hand to hand, bayonet to bayonet. We were at the border of North and South Korea, at a place called Ipack. Anyone who was in Korea knows that the heaviest and bloodiest fighting of the war took place there. There was a hill that we had to capture. We charged up, overran the enemy, and had captured the hill, but it wasn't long before we saw hundreds of the enemy swarming toward us. It was awful to see.

The Chinese had joined North Korea in the war, and hundreds of them were coming, blowing trumpets and whistles. We could see them coming from a long way off, and I was petrified with fear. There was a terrible firefight; men were falling right and left. I got shot through my arm. I started to run, then I was hit in the leg, too. Sometimes I feel ashamed that I was running, but the fear was too great. I passed out and lay there on that cold, dark hill.

When I came to I saw the Chinese going over the battlefield bayoneting the bodies to make sure they were dead. That was a routine procedure for both sides so you wouldn't get shot when your back was turned. They were going from body to body, and I waited, waited, waited for my turn. I had put my arm over my belly so the blood would make it look like I had been gut shot. They came up to me, and I lay as still as I could. They stood over me but didn't stab me. I don't know if it was because I looked too much like one of them, or if it was because of my baby face, or because they thought I'd been shot in the belly, but they passed me up.

I lay there for hours in the freezing cold with the enemy all around. I felt all my fear of dying there in that cold, faraway place, but something else, some other feelings were inside me too. I looked up at the stars and thought of the Creator and of my grandfather's stories about the beings who became the stars. I thought about that ant in the Badlands, and for the first time, I think, I really prayed.

I must have passed out again, because the next thing I knew I was lying with a bunch of wounded soldiers. Our side had retaken the hill, but I was lying with the North Korean wounded. I sat up and said, "Hey, I'm not Korean," and the medics came running over. "What's your name son?" After that they sent me back to the States to recover from my wounds. I had been in Korea for only a little more than a year, but I had seen enough to last many lifetimes.

# 5

# BLACK ROAD

Even though I was sent back to the States, it seemed like a part of me was left on that cold, dark hill in Korea. I was sent to Fitzsimmons Army Hospital to recover from my wounds. I was one of the youngest soldiers to be wounded in Korea. I spent much of my six months at Fitzsimmons in the psych ward. Most of the time I didn't know where I was, and for a long while I wasn't even able to speak. I don't think I was any better when they released me, but they must have figured I had been there long enough.

When I returned home, my father knew I was in bad shape. He took me back to Fort Berthold, where my people held a sweat for me. That sweat did more for me than all those months of therapy in the army hospital; I released a lot of my grief and fear. When I came out of that sweat I was able to talk again, and that gave me some hope. They also had an honoring ceremony for me in which I was given the name Two Ravens, an old family name on my father's side. Two Ravens was a famous chief on the Hidatsa side of my family. On his tribal records a white official changed the name to Two Crows, but this is incorrect. The name speaks of the raven, a bird my people believed to have a lot of medicine. There is a famous old portrait of him dressed in the headdress of the Dog Society. The Dog Soldiers were fearless warriors who, once they had planted their staffs, could not retreat unless another Dog Soldier released them.

A lot of veterans of the Korean and Vietnam wars came home to people who didn't honor or understand what they had gone through, and that dishonor was tough for them. The Indian people have always honored their veterans, regardless of what war they're in. Purification ceremonies are held, and the person is given a chance to speak in front of the people about what he has been through, good and bad. When I was honored by my people I felt like a human being again.

I still felt lost, though. My dad had remarried and was starting a new family. Glasgow, Montana, was not a good place for me—or for any Indian. When I went back to Fort Berthold, the Army Corps of Engineers was completing their dam across the Missouri. The story of the dam and what it did to my people needs to be told. It happened in my lifetime, not a hundred years ago. For my people it was nearly cultural genocide.

After World War II there were a lot of army engineers with nothing to do. One of the big projects the Army Corps of Engineers wanted to promote was a series of dams up and down the Missouri River. It was very convenient that most of them were to be built on Indian reservations, just above the towns and ranches of the white people. The Indians' best lands would be flooded, and the white people would get electricity, flood control, and irrigation. They would claim the right of eminent domain, which had never been used against lands that were still guaranteed by treaties. Of course, they had already stolen more than twelve million acres of land from my people that had been solemnly pledged to us at Fort Laramie. But what they wanted now was the only land we could farm. They wanted to uproot our communities and destroy our whole way of life—to destroy our valley, where we had survived for more than nine hundred years.

Our leaders fought hard against the dam but were told they had no choice in the matter, that they had better just try to get the best deal they could. A General Pick was sent to start negotiations with our tribe. At one meeting a chief named Crow Flies High, who was kind of a renegade anyway, told the general that we would never give up our valley. The general was personally insulted by the chief's "rudeness" and his lack of appreciation for the government's generous offers. General Pick said that he would never forget the insult as long as he lived and broke off the negotiations.

Even before Congress passed the act to build the dam, the Corps of Engineers was out surveying our land. People would find the stakes already set up. Our leaders pushed for the best deal they could get. All they asked for was the right to salvage our timber and water our stock from the reservoir, hunting and fishing rights, a small amount of electricity from the dam, and government assistance in moving our homes and schools and agency buildings.

At first the bill that would be signed by Congress was written up by the Bureau of Indian Affairs, but then the particulars of the bill were sent to the Corps of Engineers to be worked out. There is little doubt that it was General Pick who had a hand in the changes that were written into the final bill. In the new bill, we were denied any rights to the water for grazing or irrigation; there were no hunting and fishing rights, no free electricity, no mention of helping to rebuild our schools and roads and houses. We were even denied the right to use any of the money we received to hire lawyers to represent our claims.

Our leaders were pressured into going to Washington to sign the bill. They were told that they would receive more money if they signed right away, and that if they fought it the Three Tribes would receive no protection under the law at all. So our leaders went to Washington, where they were pressured even more. With little idea of just how bad the terms were for our people, some of our leaders signed the bill. They thought that if they didn't sign, our people would get nothing at all. They were never for it, and they knew that it could mean the end of us as a people.

From that point our land and lives were under the control of the Corps of Engineers. The dam was completed in 1956. Some of our old people didn't believe it was really happening until the water was literally up around their ankles. People were scrambling around trying to move their buildings and their livestock. The Corps wouldn't even let the People salvage the beautiful stands of timber, from which they could have built houses. The trees are still there, rotting away in the water. Some money was given for relocating their homes, but many houses didn't make the move. Our close clans and communities were destroyed as people headed to barren hills where they had landholdings. Many of our schools and community buildings were never rebuilt. Other people wound up living in trailers in the highway towns where white people controlled everything. Where there used to be big extended families, everybody went his own way; there was no longer the closeness of aunts and uncles and grandparents. Our unity was broken. The reservation was split into five pieces, and with only one bridge you have to drive hundreds of miles on bad roads around the lake to reach places that used to be just across the river.

At one time the Three Tribes had had the lowest welfare rate of any Indian tribe in the country. We had grown our own food and raised livestock. But we could no longer grow our big gardens on the dry hills. Instead of the shelter of the timber and the river for our livestock, the ones who tried to be ranchers out in the hills had to build shelters so their animals wouldn't freeze to death in the cold winds. People who used to have pure clear springs had to dig wells hundreds of feet deep to get bad water.

The government called the money given for our lands "just compensation." It didn't begin to cover what we lost. They could never pay for the trees and the berries and the fish and the animals and for our sacred places that are now underwater. There was no longer a way for most of our people to make any kind of living, and now many depend on government welfare. Many people began to drink, and there is still much alcoholism and suicide at my home. No amount of money could pay for destroying a whole way of life.

⚊⚊

While the dam was under construction, I felt there was no place for me among my people either. I was nineteen and had met a girl. We got together and went out to Washington to pick apples, but that didn't last long. About this time the government was making a big push to either terminate our reservations or get us moved into the cities so that we could forget our culture and join the "mainstream of society." On the government Relocation Program, they would send us to a city and give us a little money for some furniture and a couple month's rent. Many Indian people became lost in the city; they were separated from their people and their culture. Most were from out in the hills, and the city was a huge shock. Very few had much education, and most had to work for slave wages and live in the worst slums or even on the street.

I got on the program and moved to Los Angeles, where some of my people had already gone. At that time an Indian with a fifth-grade education who didn't know how to read had a hard time finding work, but eventually I got a job as a machinist. I did OK for a while, but I had a lot of anger inside me. There was anger and racism all around me in the streets of Los Angeles, too. I was still having nightmares about Korea, and I began to realize that even though I had fought and earned medals in a white man's war, on the streets I was just another "dirty Injun."

I started drifting around to the bars where Indians went to drink. When I was sober I really wanted to try to be like a white man, but when I started drinking I wanted to be an Indian and fight. And that's what I did: I fought anybody that called me "Chief." I fought anybody for any reason. When I got short on cash I'd get a job as a sparring partner for the professional boxers.

I did meet a pretty woman at an annual powwow held in the park. Indians from reservations all over the country had come to Los Angeles on relocation. People from all these different tribes came and camped out, and there was a friendly rivalry among the tribes. I was with my relatives from up north when I saw this girl and knew I had to meet her. Her name was Molly, and she was with the people from the pueblos in New Mexico. You could say I captured her in the old way, when warriors would capture women from other tribes. We ran off together and stayed gone for two weeks. By that time we had gotten married.

Molly's relations were awfully mad when we came back. She was a well-educated young woman from one of the most respected old families at San Juan Pueblo. I'm sure they had better things in mind for her than marrying some guy from a strange tribe that couldn't even hold down a job. We went to the pueblo to meet her family. After I was there for a while the elders began to accept me. I was taken down into their kivas and saw their secret underground ceremonies. The elders told me how long ago my people and theirs had visited and traded. It was a journey that could take a year or more. They said that sometimes marriages were even arranged as a way of keeping on friendly terms. I was given a Pueblo name, Tse Koweno, which means Lightning Sun; it is just one of many things in my life that would be connected with the powers of thunder and lightning.

I had trouble living up to being married into the most respected family at San Juan. They were very strict with any of their own people who disrupted their ancient way of life. I had the blood of chiefs in me also, but I wasn't living my life like one who could be a chief. I was still drinking and managing to get into trouble. It seems that Molly's brothers would always get wind of it. She had seven brothers, and one or another of them was always coming around and trying to give me a beating.

When Molly became pregnant I convinced her that we should move back to Los Angeles and start a life of our own. In 1956 she gave birth to our son, John. For a while I tried to do my best to hold down a job and be a good family man. Then the nightmares about Korea would start again and I would wake up screaming and shaking. Sometimes I'd be walking down the street and a certain smell would remind me of the smell of death—a smell that stays with you for a long time. I started drinking again and becoming violent. Pretty soon I was staying gone for days and coming home only long enough to demand money from my wife so I could go off on another drunk.

Molly started getting sick, coughing all the time. The doctors told her she had tuberculosis, and she went into the hospital. All I knew about tuberculosis was that most people died from it. I took little Johnny and tried to raise him on my own. We had a little apartment, and I remember how Johnny used to peel the labels off all the cans of food. We never knew if we were going to eat corn or fruit cocktail. I used to cut out pictures from the funny papers for Johnny and paste them all over one wall of our bedroom, until the landlord came one day and raised hell about it and threw us out. After that, we'd sometimes have a place to live, but just as often we'd be out living on the streets.

I hadn't been much of a father to John, and pretty soon my life really went out of control. I made the rounds of the bars, drinking and fighting and chasing women. I had no respect for my life or anyone else's. People started calling me Crazy Louie because you never knew what I was going to do or when I might go off the deep end. I thought the best thing I could do as a father for Johnny was to teach him how to fight, so no one could get the best of him, so he could survive on the streets. All I really did was show him all the anger that was inside me. I told him to be proud of being Indian, but I told him that if anyone asked him about it, he should say, "Yeah, I'm an Indian. You wanna make something of it?" I even arranged fights for him with bigger kids, until he could whip every kid around.

I was a crazy father. We were living in Compton, where Johnny was one of the few nonblack kids in his school, and he was getting picked on a lot. I went over to the school and talked to the principal about it, but he didn't have much to say. I went out of his office and pulled the fire alarm. When everyone was lined up, I went up and down the line of kids and told them I'd personally give them a whipping if they picked on my son, and if their parents had a problem with it, I'd take them on too. John wasn't bothered after that, but he never knew what his father was going to do.

John was in a karate class, and once I showed up drunk and tried to take on his teacher, who proceeded to throw me around the room. I felt ashamed in front of my son, but that was what I thought I needed to show John—that you had to show the world how tough you were. I think it helped him survive living on the streets, but it wasn't love that I showed him.

I felt really helpless about Molly. She was in the hospital for a long time, and I used my wife's sickness as another of my many excuses to drink and raise hell. I got mixed up with an Indian bunch called the White Port Gang. It wasn't much different from the gangs you hear about now. We kept guns and knives around and fought with other gangs: whites, Chicanos, blacks, even other Indians. I know now that it was one of the many times in my life when the Great Spirit was protecting me, in spite of the wrongness of my ways.

In the early 1960s Molly was put into a sanitarium, where they were trying to get her well enough to have an operation to remove part of her lungs. Johnny wasn't supposed to be in her room, and I'd have to hold Johnny up over a hedge. They could only touch their fingers, and Johnny would cry for his mom. I felt terrible.

After she had the operation, some of Molly's relatives told me she didn't make it through, just so I'd be out of her life. Molly did survive, but it was easier to believe she hadn't. Molly's relations had taken John, and I just got out of there. I thought that with all my anger and drinking, I could only hurt people, so I pretended I didn't care and hit the road.

I started wandering all over the country: down to Phoenix, over to Texas, up to Minnesota. Sometimes I would call up my relations and tell them to send a plane ticket so I could come home and sober up, and then I'd cash in the ticket and go on a big long drunk. The Indians I hung around with drank gang fashion, passing the bottle and chugging it down as fast as we could so we'd already be good and drunk if the cops showed up and hauled us in. I can remember some crazy times, and some good times, too, standing around using the hood of a car for a drum and singing Forty-niner songs—songs about women and trouble and good times.

But the good times never lasted long. Soon I would become a crazy man and get into all kinds of trouble. Then

I'd have to sober up to the fact that I was only a rotten drunk who cared only for himself. There were things I had watched my drinking relatives do that I had sworn I would never do. I had sworn I would never hit a woman, yet I did.

A few years later, I wound up in Denver. There I started to pull my life together and got a decent job. By then, I had found out that Molly was still alive, and I wanted a second chance. I smooth-talked Molly into bringing John to Denver and trying to start over. But after a while I started drinking again, and my mental and physical abuse became too much for them. Molly and John got on a bus and went back to her people. John was twelve years old, and it would be years before I would see him again. I never saw Molly again.

# 6

# THE ANGRY WARRIOR

I was wandering around up north, and I went over to Montana to see my father. I had long hair then, all the way down my back. My father told me that when I wore my hair like that it meant something, that whether I knew it or not I was representing my Indian people. When I drank and fought and acted crazy, people wouldn't think, "There's a guy with big problems." They would say, "There's another drunk Indian."

I thought a lot about that. I told myself I'd quit fighting and being a crazy man. One day I was in a bar and some cowboy started calling me "Chief." Before I knew it, I was out in the street beating the heck out of him. Later, I was really ashamed. The next day I went to the barber and had all my hair cut off. I grew a mustache and looked like a Mexican. Then they could call me "Pancho" or anything else, anything but an Indian.

In 1966 I went to Chicago, back on the Relocation Program. I was still trying to live in two worlds, and I wasn't making it in either one. When I moved to Chicago I thought I was going to do my best to fit into the white man's world. I was going to sober up and try to find a decent job. I would save up my money and get a nice car, nice clothes, and all the things a person in white society is supposed to want. I would start over again in the white man's world.

I did manage to stay sober and hold down a job for quite a while, then suddenly I found myself on a big drunk and out on the streets again. All my money was gone.

About that time, there started to be more and more talk in the Indian community about "Red Power"—about standing up for our rights as nations within a nation, our rights to have our own culture and way of life, which the government had tried for so long to destroy. Stands were being made out on some of the reservations: the fight for fishing rights of the Northwest tribes, the struggle back east on the Iroquois lands, where they wanted to build yet another dam. Many of the Indians who were relocated to the cities felt that the government had tried to take everything Indian from them their whole lives and then abandoned them in the city, where they were supposed to assimilate into a strange culture. Groups in the cities began to share and learn about Native culture and to work for better treatment for the Indians that were struggling there.

I was living on the streets again when one of these groups took me in and gave me a place to stay. They called themselves "Indians for Indians." They started organizing protests and demonstrations, and I would tag along. One time they took over the harbor on Lake Michigan. For many months they had an Indian village set up by Cub Stadium. They were trying to establish a cultural center, a place where people could go to get off the streets. It was good to see my Indian people starting to stand up for themselves, but I wasn't serious about anything back then. I thought I had too many of my own problems to deal with. When I look back on my time with Indians for

Indians, I think that maybe I was just trying to get my picture in the paper.

After a while I moved to Minneapolis, in 1968, right at the founding of the American Indian Movement. The streets of Minneapolis are still one of the toughest places for Indians to survive, and the ones who started the movement were guys who had survived the streets and the white man's boarding schools and his prisons and his military. Some had been adopted out to white families and had to completely relearn their culture. But in the prisons and other places they had been doing their homework. They learned about the history of genocide that this country was founded on, and they woke up to the fact that the genocide never ended. When the government couldn't exterminate us and we didn't disappear, it was decided that at all costs we had to be assimilated into white society. For many Native people, assimilation is the same as genocide.

At first AIM was getting some money from the churches and the state for programs to help people find housing and jobs. AIM had its own neighborhood patrols to find places for the drunks and street people before the cops could get to them and beat them up and throw them in jail. They set up "survival schools" where kids could learn about their own culture, as well as learning how to survive in the white man's world. AIM always taught that we should look to the elders; we should go back to the elders to learn the culture and to seek their advice. AIM brought the elders into the survival schools.

AIM had its leaders, but it was a very loose organization. It was a grass-roots movement; there weren't any memberships or formal leadership. Right from the start there were guys who would put on a red headband and an AIM jacket and come around drinking or just causing trouble for everybody and using AIM as an excuse for their craziness. Pretty soon there was a push from Clyde

Bellecourt, Dennis Banks, and others for the people that called themselves AIM to clean up their act. "Don't come around if you're drinking. Our people need real warriors, not a bunch of drunks and dopers and crazies."

That was a start for me. I didn't drink when I was involved in AIM activities, even though I still snuck around at other times. And I was getting back my pride in being Native American. I knew the whole history of how my own people had suffered at the hands of the white man, and I was learning how all over the country assaults were still being made on our land and culture. I was learning how the Bureau of Indian Affairs, which had been set up to look after the interests and the treaty rights of the Indian people, had instead become an agency whose goal was to serve the white men that wanted our land and minerals. The U.S. government took away the power of our chiefs and set up the tribal councils that became their puppet governments. I had been trained to fight in a white man's war, but once again my own people were up against the country I had fought for. That caused a lot of bitterness in me. But now there was something I could fight for and that I could believe in.

In the early 1970s AIM was getting involved with the Lakota nation's struggle for the return of the Black Hills— Paha Sapa, the sacred center of the Lakota world. The Black Hills had been solemnly sworn to the Lakota by the Fort Laramie Treaty of 1868. Six years later, General Custer led an expedition that confirmed rumors of gold in the Black Hills, and the miners started to pour in. The government tried to get the Lakotas to sell the Black Hills for a ridiculous price. It wasn't long before there was strong pressure on the government to take the Black Hills by force. From then on, any Lakota bands that weren't on a reservation and wouldn't agree to the cheap sale of their sacred Black Hills would be considered hostile. In June 1876 the "hostiles" took out their frustrations at the Battle of Little Big Horn, when Custer attacked their village. Then the full weight of the government was turned toward breaking the Lakotas' resistance. In the end Crazy Horse and Sitting Bull were both murdered, and the power of the Lakotas seemed to be broken forever when more than two hundred unarmed men, women, and children were massacred at Wounded Knee in 1890.

When uranium deposits were discovered on Lakota reservation land in the 1950s, the government began offering money once again. The traditional Lakotas said that their sacred land was not for sale, just as they had always insisted. At this same time, the big energy corporations were looking to turn the Black Hills and the nearby reservation land into what AIM called a "national sacrifice area," stripping them of the coal and oil and uranium they know is there. Half of the gold that the United States mined and hoarded had already come from the Black Hills, and now industry and the military wanted to complete the rape of the Paha Sapa. The traditional Lakotas and even AIM didn't know all of this at first; they were only looking for the solemn promises in the Fort Laramie Treaty to be honored. They held protests on top of the presidents' faces that had been carved into a sacred mountain taken from the Lakotas. After the Trail of Broken Treaties march and takeover of the BIA (Bureau of Indian Affairs) building in Washington in November 1972, the government began to consider AIM a top priority for elimination. The problem wasn't the protests, it was that AIM was helping to wake up the Indian people to the government's ongoing oppression. The invaders weren't keen on the idea that their own treaties should be honored.

⟿

Another source of anger and bitterness for Native Americans is the racism and injustice that surround them. The Indian people are looked down on and discriminated against, and some of the worst racists are white people who profit from the Indians in the stores and through cheap land leases and other ways. In many western states there is a huge number of Native prisoners, completely out of proportion to the percentage of Indian people living in those states. Indians are thrown into prison over and over, while white crimes against Indians aren't even prosecuted.

While AIM was getting involved in the Black Hills issue there was a murder in February 1972 in the reservation border town of Gordon, Nebraska. A quiet fifty-one-year-old homeless man named Raymond Yellow Thunder was badly beaten by two white brothers, who then stripped off his clothes and paraded him around in front of a crowd at a local American Legion dance. After they drove him around in their trunk for a while, they dumped Raymond off in the street; a couple of days later he died. The town was going to sweep it under the rug; the brothers were going to go free. Raymond's family wasn't allowed to see his body or the autopsy report, and the family finally called on AIM to help them see that justice was done. I was part of a huge caravan of AIM people who arrived in Gordon to find a whole troop of law enforcement officers waiting to meet us. They finally agreed to the demands that the two brothers be put on trial.

In Custer, South Dakota, AIM showed up to demand another white man be brought to justice in the January 1973 stabbing of Wesley Bad Heart Bull. This time the police were ready with all their riot gear. They let only a few AIM people into the courthouse to talk, but they wouldn't let Wesley's mother in. Instead they teargassed her and beat her on the steps. That started their riot; it ended with the courthouse being burned.

AIM was starting to get the respect of some of the Lakota elders because they were willing to act instead of just talk about what was wrong. At the same time many people in AIM, including myself, were looking to the Lakota elders for spiritual guidance. I had grown up with the traditional ways, but a lot of the people in AIM had grown up in the cities or had been apart from their culture most of their lives. When they returned to the reservations, they began to relearn their own cultural and spiritual ways. At the same time, they were helping the traditional people on the reservations take action against the injustices that were a part of their daily lives and helping them to feel the pride and courage they needed to stand up for the things they believed in. The Sun Dance, which had been outlawed for many years, was brought out in the open again, and many of the AIM people became sun dancers and went into the sweat lodges.

For a long time the traditionals and full-blood Lakotas had been kept down by government programs and tribal policies that favored the mixed-bloods and the ones who were for progress the white man's way. When Dick Wilson was elected tribal chairman of Pine Ridge reservation, the government had found a yes-man for their policies, such as giving up even more Lakota land for uranium mining. Wilson vowed to chase AIM and all the outside "communist agitators" off the reservation. With government money and support and guns he put together his own little private army made up of his relations and his drinking buddies, and they began to terrorize the traditionals and anyone that disagreed with his policies. Just about every day there was a drive-by shooting, someone beat up by his thugs, or a body found out on the prairie. Even the elders and little children were being terrorized. Wilson even named his private army the "goons"—Guardians of the Oglala Nation.

One time I was at a home in Oglala; it was nighttime, and there was a gathering with women and kids around.

All of a sudden bullets were flying all over the house. Someone was shooting into the house where all those people were gathered. Amazingly, no one was even wounded that night, and the goons finally took off. I still believe that it was because of the power of Billy Good Voice Elk, who was there that night. He was a powerful man who carried the pipe for Crazy Horse's band of people (his *tiyoshpaye*). Crazy Horse kept a powerful medicine that could keep away bullets.

Dick Wilson's abuse of his powers and his harassment of the traditional Lakota people was getting worse by the day. In 1973 it was decided that a stand had to be made. Some of the traditional Lakotas called on AIM to come and help them. Dick Wilson had the tribal headquarters set up like a fortress; he was expecting a battle right in town. Instead the People went to Wounded Knee, which is just a little outpost on the prairie with a couple of stores and a church; but a monument there marks where more than two hundred unarmed men, women, and children were massacred in 1890. This was Big Foot's peaceful band of Ghost Dancers, who were promised they would be brought into Pine Ridge safely. The Lakota will never forget what happened there.

This little outpost, Wounded Knee, couldn't have meant much to the government, but pretty soon the people that took over Wounded Knee were surrounded by a huge army of military and FBI and goons, with every kind of tank and high-tech weapon. Media people from all over the world showed up. But the People there had put on the *tokala*, the red paint, to show their determination to lay down their lives if they had to. I was one of those who received the paint from Leonard Crow Dog. Two of the defenders of Wounded Knee did pay that price: Frank Clearwater and Buddy Lamont, a young Lakota man who was buried beside the mass grave where the frozen bodies of Big Foot's people were heaped up by the soldiers after the first Wounded Knee massacre.

For two months we held out against the might of the U.S. government. The law enforcement men and the goons were all for going in and taking us out, starting a second Wounded Knee massacre. I remember the bravery of ones like Oscar Bear Runner, Leonard Crow Dog, Carter Camp, and all the people there, from the men on security to the women who kept everything going with bullets flying all around. I remember the ceremonies that were held there. When it was cold at night on patrol, I'd feel like I was right back in Korea again. There's nothing great about what I did there. I was in and out of "the Knee," helping run supplies in. I did take a little pride in slipping right past the goons at night. I was within ten yards of those guys without their seeing or hearing me—and they were Indians!

To end the siege, the government made a lot of promises about all the issues, such as the Black Hills, that they would look into. After the people walked out of Wounded Knee, none of the promises were kept; but for a while the attention of the whole world was drawn to a little spot on the prairie where a small bunch of Native people held out against a mighty superpower.

During the 1970s the FBI was calling AIM the most violent terrorist group in the country, yet any arms we had and the stands we made were only in defense against the many threats being made toward the land and the lives and the rights of the Indian nations. Many AIM members had been trained as Green Berets and in special forces units; Indians were known for taking the toughest assignments in the military. It was sometimes said as a boast that we could bring this country to its knees in twenty-four hours. We could have bombed bridges and power plants and buildings, but we didn't. We never did any of those things.

It's hard to understand why little groups like AIM and the Black Panthers were such a threat to the mightiest nation in the world. I think it was because the government didn't want the citizens to be reminded of the history of genocide and slavery. The Black Panthers and AIM both stood against the idea of being assimilated into the white man's world; they dared to question the American Dream. And of course the government considered it a real problem to have the Native people of this land waking up and asking that the treaties and promises be kept, and wanting to control their own land and their own lives.

There is nothing special about what I did in AIM. I never wanted to be a leader. I usually worked security. After I took the red face-paint, though, I knew I could be called to go anywhere in the country where my Indian people were making a stand. One place was Big Mountain in Arizona, the home and the sacred female mountain of a very traditional group of Diné (Navajo) people. The government wanted to evict thousands of self-sufficient Diné from their homes and move them to government housing, with the approval of the Hopi and Navajo tribal councils. In the 1980s the government started impounding the People's sheep and tearing up the land, building huge fences and roads. The Diné knew that it would be the end of their culture if they moved off their land and accepted government handouts. The land was Hopi, according to lines the government drew up a hundred years ago, but most of the traditional Hopis wanted to leave the Diné be. Once again, though, the government had Indians fighting Indians—the same divide-and-conquer tactics the white man had used against us for centuries.

And once again there was the question of why the government was so interested in an intertribal dispute over a piece of desert land where the Diné raised their sheep. The Hopi tribal council had already leased land at Black Mesa for a huge strip mine, and there was a lot of coal under Big Mountain, too. The traditional Diné and Hopis believe that that is what the government was interested in. The women elders, the Diné grandmothers, led the way in standing up to the BIA police and federal marshals that were trying to evict them. They went out and cut the fences the government tried to put up to keep their sheep from grazing.

The only time the Sun Dance was taken out of the Great Plains was in support of the Diné at Big Mountain. Leonard Crow Dog led the dance. People from many different tribes danced for four days there in the hot sand. Any AIM members who weren't dancing were working security, keeping the dance from being disrupted and watching for the feds. We had bunkers set up around the Sun Dance grounds, and somehow we got a hold of the codes the Navajo police and the feds were using, so we always knew what they were up to.

The government had set a deadline of July 7, 1986, for the Diné to move off their land. It was the day after the fourth Sun Dance at Big Mountain ended. I was with the veterans of World War II, Korea, and Vietnam who marched together with the Diné grandmothers and children, who were armed only with sticks and rocks. We marched to where the government had built a huge fence and started cutting it down. Someone had just cut some of the barbed wire and handed it to me. I held it up in my raised fist just as a photographer snapped a picture of me. That picture went out to newspapers all over the country. The march stopped the forced relocation of the Diné.

I was pretty paranoid for a while after that picture was flashed all across the country. All of AIM's leaders had been either in jail or on trial, and the government had infiltrators that tried to disrupt the movement as much as possible. Even some of our own Indian people believed the government's line about AIM being a bunch of crazy terrorists. Many tribal council people denounced AIM— and the same people are now benefiting from and even taking credit for the gains that were made because of the stands that AIM took.

There are people at my home in Fort Berthold who still remember me as a "crazy militant," and I did a lot of crazy things in those days. One time when I was at home the police wanted to question me about guns or something. I told them that right at that moment I had explosives planted in the police station and snipers had them in their sights. Of course it wasn't true, but they let me walk away. That's how fearful all the media coverage about the "terrorist" American Indian Movement made people.

More and more the government that I had once fought for became my enemy. "White man" was always a political term for AIM, signifying the people in power that kept people oppressed all over the world. We used the term even though many white people helped our cause in many ways. For me, though, all the anger and bitterness inside me became directed against the "white world," the dominant culture, which was practically the whole world I was living in. There was no way to escape it. I worked with and went to school with and was around white people all the time, and it was hard to walk around with all that anger.

Fear fed that anger, too. A lot of people had paid the ultimate price for being activists. One day an AIM buddy and I were driving out of the little town of Scenic, South Dakota, when a big black car with aerials all over it pulled up behind us. You could tell the men inside were government law enforcement officers. All of a sudden bullets were flying; they were on our tail and shooting at us. We finally lost them on a gravel road that went off into the Badlands. When we stopped I was really shook up. I felt like I was back in Korea, except this time the people shooting were the same people I had fought for over there. I started on a big drunk, and my friends could tell I was in a bad way. I was taken to a sweat where we are taught to pray for our enemies, and they prayed there for the hatred to leave me. But it didn't leave for a long time.

During that whole time, back in my militant days, only one incident went on my permanent police record although I was in jail more than once. They still use this one incident to make it hard for me to get into the prisons, where I'm trying to help Native prisoners in their fight to have the sweat lodge and the instruments of worship. I was in Rapid City getting a motel room for a white man who was helping the movement. An old Lakota couple was trying to get a room, and the desk clerk told them that there were no more rooms left. The next couple was white, and the desk clerk rented them a room. This is the kind of racist treatment that the Lakota people had grown to expect. Since I was with a white guy, they rented us a room, but I was mad by that time. I put another room on the credit card then went out and found four old drinking buddies who were living on the streets and told them they could have a motel room to sleep in for the night. I guess they trashed the room pretty badly, and the motel pressed charges on me for it.

It took a long time for me to deal with the fear and anger, the thoughts of revenge against white society. I am still dedicated to the American Indian Movement and the things it is still fighting for. I still have anger over the policies of the U.S. government. But my thoughts of revenge had to be replaced by wanting to be a positive force for change. The American Indian Movement is still very much alive, but now you can find the leaders praying in the sweat lodge and the ceremonies more than out demonstrating. When the people in AIM started going back to the reservations and started searching for their spiritual roots, they found that in our true teachings we must pray for all peoples, even our enemies; that we must pray for "all our relations," which includes everything and everyone on this earth. Now it's more of a spiritual war we are fighting, and it's for the survival of the Mother Earth, of life itself.

Make no mistake, though, there are still those of us who would be willing to lay down our lives for our people. But there are plenty of problems right in the Indian communities, such as alcoholism and teen suicide; there's a lot of work to do. There's still a lot of educating of the non-Indian people in this country that needs to be done. Very few know that we have our own Indian nations, our own spiritual ways, our own languages, that we are people who might be offended if others use paint and feather headdresses and the drum, things that are sacred to us, and use them to cheer on the Redskins and the Chiefs.

My people don't need handouts. We don't want to be charity cases. A partner of mine in AIM used to say, "Don't give us your cast-off clothes and things. If you're going to give us clothes, give us some nice new ones with the tags still on them." What we want is self-determination and to be self-sufficient.

We will need another generation that can match some of the true warriors I have known in AIM. The struggle for our rights as nations will not end. The government and the big companies know that under what they thought was worthless land is much of this country's coal and uranium and oil. AIM put a halt to some of the big companies' plans to strip the reservations of their resources, to turn them into "national sacrifice areas," but it will come up again and again.

≈

There is one of our leaders who never made it out of prison. In 1996 Leonard Peltier will have sat in prison for twenty years for the alleged murder of two FBI agents.

After Wounded Knee things got even worse at Pine Ridge. Dick Wilson and the goons were out for revenge, and the reservation was crawling with FBI agents. The FBI was supplying the goons with guns and ammunition and all the booze they needed to be brave enough to go out and harass the traditional Lakota people. Almost every day the drive-by shootings and beatings and unsolved murders went on. Even the elders and little children were being terrorized.

Many of the People wanted to form an independent Oglala nation, to be free of Dick Wilson, to make their own decisions, to stand for the return of the Black Hills, and to help their communities. Once again a call went out from the elders to AIM to help protect the traditional Lakota. The AIM members who came worked together with the Lakota; they started community gardens, schools, and programs for the elders. The AIM people stayed on even though their lives were constantly in danger. Just about everyone on the reservation had to go around armed at all times. After Wounded Knee, Dick Wilson had vowed to chase AIM off the reservation by whatever means it took.

Leonard Peltier came to Pine Ridge when the call went out to help the Lakota people there; he was always wherever he was needed to help out. He fixed cars, he helped out the elders, he did whatever needed to be done. In 1975 a group of AIM people were staying on the little ranch of an old couple named the Jumping Bulls. The FBI had the place figured as a heavily armed camp of terrorists. They had maps of bunkers that were really only root cellars and dirt piles. One morning two FBI agents drove into the place supposedly looking for a young kid who had stolen a pair of boots; they had already been chased off without a warrant the day before. Maybe a warning shot was fired, or maybe they fired a shot as some kind of signal, but for some reason the FBI agents got out of their car and started firing into the houses. The women and children were gotten out of there, and a firefight began. It's very strange why these agents would get out of their car and start shooting into houses where they knew there were women and children, and why they didn't retreat when they had plenty of opportunities, but the agents were finally wounded and someone went down and finished them off.

Somehow the law knew that something was going to happen, because within an hour there were hundreds of law enforcement officers on the scene. Maybe they were even willing to sacrifice two of their agents as an excuse to go in and wipe out the AIM supporters. Leonard and a group of them, under heavy fire, somehow escaped into the prairie; those people say they had seen an eagle lead the way to their escape. A huge manhunt was on. The government spent millions of dollars to track down the people that were defending their camp, even though there were then over a hundred, some say over three hundred, unsolved murders on Pine Ridge that were never investigated. Some of the press was even saying that the agents had been scalped by the "terrorists" after they ambushed them.

After a while Dino Butler and Bob Roubidou were put on trial as being Leonard's accomplices in murdering the agents. A jury in Iowa said that there wasn't enough evidence to know how the agents were killed and that the people had acted in self-defense. Leonard had fled to Canada, and the FBI wanted him very badly; they had to have someone to take the rap. They got Canada to extradite him back to the States. This time they got a cooperative judge and held the trial in North Dakota, which is one of the worst places in this country for an Indian to get justice. All kinds of defense evidence that the FBI had coerced people and tampered with evidence was thrown out by the judge. Leonard got two consecutive life sentences.

Leonard's appeals have been denied over and over again. Now the government has a political prisoner on its hands, and all over the world, whenever the United States talks about human rights and political prisoners, there are people who will say, "What about Leonard Peltier?" But the FBI wanted to punish someone they thought was a leader. And Leonard *is* a leader, but not in the way they think. He is a leader because he is humble and puts the People before himself; that's the way he has always been. When I go to visit Leonard he doesn't talk about the violent overthrow of the government. He talks about our young ones and how to get them off of alcohol and drugs, how to make opportunities for our people so they can stand on their own; he talks about the future of our people. And he still likes to laugh and joke around.

We thought Leonard would be out in five years at the most. Then, from 1983 to 1986 we danced the Sun Dance at the Jumping Bull property to pray for Leonard and our people in prison. Steve Roubidou, Leonard's cousin, put on that Sun Dance; he is one that has never quit fighting for Leonard's release, and for the struggles of our people. If I could, I would trade places with Leonard now. I would say, "Let me take some of this punishment that never ends." Leonard is strong, but he is in poor health, and I know the years are weighing heavy on him. All he wants is to live like a normal human being again.

For a while now I've been Leonard's spiritual advisor; I am supposed to help him to find the strength he needs in our spiritual ways. Not long ago Leonard was at the federal medical center near where I live, and I visited him there to do a pipe ceremony. He was in pain from his longtime health problems. The guards led Leonard in with handcuffs on so tight they were cutting his wrists. Three guards had to stand over this peaceful man, and he had to smoke our sacred pipe with handcuffs on. The guards refused to take them off. As I said, I am supposed to help Leonard find strength in our spiritual ways, but this was almost more than either of us could take. I felt shame for those that could treat a human being that way.

The bottom line is the government. They put him in there no matter how they had to do it, and now they must set him free for the good of everyone, for the healing between the invaders and the Native People to begin. It's up to the president now. What is one man? If the government needs to prove a point, the point has been proven. Now set this man free. *

---

* For donations or information please contact the Leonard Peltier Defense Council, P.O. Box 583, Lawrence, Kansas 66044. Phone: (913) 842-5774.

# 7

# FILLING IN THE HOLES

When I look at my own life I know that it is possible for anyone to change with the help of the ancient ways. My grandfather said that we are all born holy, but through our life we experience different things, and we forget that we are a part of the balance, one with the Creation. The Old Ones said that the first thing a baby can hear in its mother's womb is the heartbeat of the Mother Earth, and the little one will hear it in the drum at the powwows and ceremonies. We can still hear it in the drum, and there is a part of us that never forgets our oneness with the Creation.

I had found a reason to live in the fight for the survival of my people, and I had even begun to relearn something of our spiritual ways, but there was still much anger inside of me. I would still fall off the wagon and get myself into trouble and hurt others. I had spent many years using my wife's sickness, and the war, and anger at the white man as an excuse to drink. I lied and I used my own people. Every time I would do these things I would tell myself, "Well, I've done the worst, it can never be that bad again," and the next time it would be worse than before.

I remember well the day my grandfather passed away. Before the burial there is a feast for the one who passed on and an all-night vigil of the ones who wish to honor him. Late that night I went out under the stars, and suddenly I felt my grandfather's spirit right there with me. I could feel his presence, just like when I was young and he'd sit beside me on that big rock in the creek and not say anything. It made me feel good.

For a long time after that my thoughts would go back to my grandfather and the things he taught. These things made me want to change, but I lacked the courage. I knew that people are very slow to forget the kinds of things I had done; my own people have a very long memory. It was then I remembered and began to understand a teaching my grandfather had given me when I was just a kid.

When I was growing up, my cousin and I were always getting into some kind of trouble. Grandpa would tell us not to rope and ride the calves because they were too young and we could hurt them. There was a bluff over the creek behind his place that we always jumped off of, even though Grandpa warned us about it all the time. We always thought that Grandpa never knew we'd been riding those poor calves and doing all those things that we knew he'd get on us about.

One day, though, Grandpa took us back to a little spot out behind the granaries where he stored the corn and the wheat that he farmed. I can still see him with his big white hat as he kneeled down and started to sharpen a willow stick. He took a rock and pounded the willow stick into the ground and said that from now on whenever we did something we knew we shouldn't do, we should pound a stake into the ground. "And knowing you guys," he said, "you're going to be cutting a lot of stakes."

But then he told us that every time we were about to do something we knew was bad, and then kept ourselves from doing it, we could pull out one of the stakes. My cousin and I each had our line of stakes. "Now, only you guys will know how many stakes you have. I won't ever come out here. This will be your place. You will be the only ones who will know."

For a while we were faithful about pounding a stake in when we knew we did something wrong. But after a while it became a game for us. We'd think about bad stuff to do, and then not do it just so we could pull up a stake.

One day we were feeling proud of ourselves because we had both pulled up all our stakes, and we ran off to find Grandpa. We finally found him and said, "Grandpa, come and see. We've been really good, and all our stakes are pulled up."

Grandpa didn't say anything. He just walked slowly out to our little place and acted like he was studying the ground very carefully. "Good, good job. I'm proud of you guys. You pulled up all your stakes. But I still see something there."

We looked at the ground and said, "Oh, you mean those holes. We can just cover them up."

Grandpa said, "I see the holes there, but you can't cover them up so easily. When you put the hole in the ground, you hurt our Mother. And when you do those things I tell you not to do, you put a little hole in my heart. As you go through life, if you're not living in a good way you will put holes in the hearts of people, even the ones you love, and people will never forget these things. But there is a way you can begin to fill in the holes.

"These holes you put into our Mother. You can pull the stakes out, but it takes time to fill in these holes. After time has passed, and the wind and the rain and the passing animals and the dust come along, these holes will start to fill. That is the way in your life; time will pass, and those things you have done will begin to fade. But if you live in such a way that your mind and your heart and your speech and your actions are one, and are of service to your people; if the people begin to say, "He used to be that way, but now he walks a good road," then maybe you can come back and finish filling in some of those holes. It's not your words but your actions that help to fill in the holes. Changing helps to fill in the holes. Remember, it's not what you say you are, but what the People say you are." Grandpa got up and slowly walked away, and we sat there just staring at the holes we had made in the Earth.

As we travel around the Medicine Wheel, the Sacred Circle of Life, we will come to an obstacle or a hole; it may be something that comes from our childhood, or a difficulty, or some way we have treated others. Many people will try to go around it—you might go off and find a new religion or a new relationship or something—but we will always stumble into that hole again. I believe it is possible for anyone to turn his life around, but filling in the holes takes longer. As we begin to fill them in we can begin our spiritual walk.

We can never deny where we came from or forget the things we have done or that others have done to us, but as we learn to live in the balance we discover ways to begin to fill in the holes. The past is just shadow memories, but they are very real at the same time. These shadows follow us around and can cause a lot of pain. But you will get to where you can pick yourself up and begin to walk the circle, learning and growing once more.

I had left many holes along my path, and I would create many more. Many holes I would never fill. It would be years before I truly began to walk a spiritual road, before I found my sobriety. There was too much anger and fear and hurt and ways that I hurt others, but in my grandfather's teachings I found a way that I could begin to be whole again. He taught that the true path of the warrior is to face our greatest enemy, the one within ourselves. That is how we begin. A lot of time would pass before I found I had a great ally.

# 8

# THE GIFT

Not many people know about my short career as an evangelical preacher. I don't tell many people about it, but once in a while Crow Dog or someone who knew me back then still calls me "Rev." As I began to remember the good teachings of my grandfather and the others who gave me the courage to begin to turn my life around, I also started to seek a spiritual direction. I still committed to my people's struggles, I began going to the sweat lodges, Sun Dances, and other ceremonies, which were being brought out in the open and growing stronger all the time. I had my grandfather's teachings, and I could remember when my own people were self-sufficient and strong in their spiritual ways.

Maybe our ways were growing stronger, but Indian people were still the poorest in the country and still being victimized every day. I was looking for some spiritual answers, and I began to wonder about this religion of the white man. I was talking about it to my father once. I said that behind his God the white man had conquered this whole hemisphere, and this country was

71

the most powerful on earth. I knew that there is only one
God, one Creator, but what was it that made their way of
worship so powerful?

My father had spent a lot of his life trying to make it
in the white man's world; he had been through the boarding schools and mission schools where Christianity was
forced on my people. Yet he never became a Christian
and still believed strongly that the old ways of our own
people were good. But a lot of my Mandan, Hidatsa, and
Arickara people had become Christians. Our traditional
people have always believed that all the ways of worship-
ing the Great Spirit have truth in them. My father knew
I needed something in my life, and he thought that if I
was looking for answers about the white man's way of
worship, that I should go to a place where they teach about
the white man's God and his son, Jesus. He even went to
the tribal chairman and asked if I could get a scholarship
to a Christian college.

In 1974 I went to a six-week Bible study program at a
college in Florida. By listening to tapes I learned all about
the white man's book. And I will tell you, there are many
good and beautiful things in there, such as the proverbs of
Solomon. There is much beauty and wisdom in those
words.

Part of our Bible school studies included going
around to some of the churches to see how they conducted their services. They sent me and another Indian student to a Pentecostal church. The preacher was
walking back and forth and swinging his arms around.
At one point he rolled up his sleeves and showed the
people the marks on his arms where he had been a
dopehead. The people started to stand up and shout,
and pretty soon this fellow next to me fell down and I
thought he was having a seizure. Others were dancing
around and the preacher was doing healings. He would
hit people on the head and *bam!* they'd fall flat on their

backs. My friend and I looked at each other and thought, "Man, these white people are violent," and started heading for the door. A man stopped us and told us to stay, that these people were just "in the spirit." We wound up staying and seeing it through. Later I would go to other "Holy Roller" churches and got fairly used to it.

I didn't realize it, but I started to develop a "holier-than-thou" attitude. I would look at someone and think, "Oh, he's smoking, he must be an adulterer too." After a while I became a pretty good talker about the Bible, and I gave a good talk on TV one time. I saw that all the other preachers had nice suits and clothes, and I wasn't going to be outdone. I bought some black slacks, a red suit coat, a white turtleneck, and a big cross on a chain. I was really sharp!

My six weeks of Bible study were up, and the people at the college were really after me to stay on and keep on preaching the gospel; they thought I was a natural. I was asked to give an important talk to a group of Baptists. I thought I knew everything I was going to talk about, and I was going to talk on forgiveness. I got up there in my new suit coat and slacks and started to speak, when suddenly a strange feeling came over me: Could I be sure I knew what I was talking about? I didn't know whether or not I was living what the Bible talked about, or whether anybody was. I worried that I might be making fun of the Creator by talking about things I didn't understand. I didn't understand what it meant to be born into sin. I didn't really know anything about this hell they talked about, or about this heaven up in the sky somewhere that was supposed to be all that we lived for. And then a powerful feeling came over me and hit me like a bolt of lightning: I had to return to the Mother, to the ways of the Earth. I tried to speak, but nothing would come out; I just stood there and couldn't say anything. The preachers onstage with me were waving their arms around, trying to signal me to get off the stage; they were really upset. I finally walked away from the pulpit, and that was the end of my days as a preacher.

I still believe that if people truly follow the way of Jesus, it is a beautiful way of life. But I knew I could never be a preacher. I had too hard a time listening to a man up there being holier-than-thou and saying that he had no worries, and that the people would have no worries if they just gave 10 percent to the church. Even our medicine people have worries, just because they are human beings. In our ways no one is holier than another; we are all equal in spirit to the Great Spirit, and we are all born holy. In our ways we don't look for a reward in some other place, in heaven. We are given this Earth, our Mother, to care for, and we are given a life, with all its pain and joy. We grow stronger and try to learn and do our best with the short time we are given here.

⟨⟩

I wanted to start over in a place where no one knew me. I thought it would be easier to get my life back together in a place where my past wouldn't come back to haunt me. After Wounded Knee, I went on the Relocation Program again, this time to Evansville, Indiana. There were very few Indian people there, and it got pretty lonely. I remembered that even before I went to Bible school my father had told me that whenever I was troubled or lonely I should go to one of the white man's little gray houses of worship. He said that if there were fifty people in there, maybe there would be ten who would be truly praying to the Great Spirit, and I could pray with them and our prayers would be heard by the Grandfather, Tunkashila.* That is what I would do when I felt truly alone.

After a while I got a good job at a foundry. My boss liked me. When our foreman quit, my boss asked me if I wanted his job. The job paid a lot of money, and I felt honored. But then he asked me if I had a high school diploma. I had to tell him that I never made it past the fifth grade. Then he said he could arrange for me to study and get my GED. That guy really treated me well.

I decided I would go for it; except for the big problem that I couldn't read. Illiteracy was part of the reason I wound up in Korea; it's why I never could find a decent job, and it lowered my self-esteem. But I didn't know how I could even begin. I started to get some tutoring. Then I would just walk around all the time and try to read everything: store signs, street signs, the labels on cans. I started to notice that the words I saw stayed in my brain. I read and read anything with words until I was reading books. Eventually I took that GED test and aced it. I ended up getting a state achievement award for the best score. It was hard to believe.

It was then I remembered something that had happened when I was young. I had drawn a picture of a mountain, and somehow I had written the words WHITE MOUNTAIN at the top, even though I couldn't read. One of my uncles told my grandfather what I had written. Grandpa called me over and told me that I really captured that mountain

---

*Creator, Great Spirit, Great Mystery, are names used by many Native Americans to speak of the all-pervading creator and sustainer of the universe. *Tunkashila* is a Lakota word for "grandfather," used in addressing that aspect of the deity that can hear the prayers of and intercede on behalf of humankind. In a culture that stresses the relatedness of all things, Tunkashila/Grandfather denotes a relationship between humankind and the Creator. It doesn't necessarily confine the deity to any concept of form or gender, for as the Great Mystery, the deity is believed to be beyond any such human conceptions. *[RL]*

in my mind. "Now, you can keep drawing the things in
your mind, and if you keep it up you will draw something
really good, something that will make the people see what
you see in your mind. As for the words that you wrote on
your picture, I think there is a gift here. I feel that you
will use it to help your people; you will do something
good with this gift. Someday you will be a chief and help
your people." It made me feel proud when he said that.
He didn't mean that someday I would necessarily be a
powerful leader. He meant that someday I might earn the
honor of my people. Many things my grandfather told me
I began to understand only much later in my life.

I did so well on my GED that I received a letter asking
me if I wanted to attend the University of Southern Indiana. This was in 1976. At first I laughed at the thought of
an Indian with a fifth-grade education going to college,
but I began to think that maybe I could learn something
there to help myself and my people. It took a lot of courage for me to walk into a college classroom for the first
time. Then I remembered that ant in the Badlands, and
that ant helped me once more, helped me to overcome
my fears. I was taking psychology classes and learning
interesting things. I read books by psychologists such as
Abraham Maslow that said many of the same things that
were taught by my people. I told my professor how my
people would take someone who was having problems and
build a fire at night. They would have the person act out
his problems in front of the flames; whatever his frustrations were, or if he had committed a crime or beat his
children or whatever, he acted it out and was told to give
it to the fire. His people would be around him but he
wouldn't be able to see them, only the fire. Today they
would call it psychodrama.

I remember a young woman among my people who
had lost her baby. She was so full of grief that no one could
help her. Finally her relations made her a little doll that

she could carry around, and she loved that doll. She would talk to that doll, and she would take it to the powwows and dance around with it. For four years she danced at the powwows with that doll, and she got to where she could be happy again. On the fourth year one of our leaders told her that now her baby could be honored with a name and could go on to its home with the Great Spirit. That woman gave him the doll and they put it away and gave the baby a spirit name, and that woman was healed of her grief. There are all kinds of ways that our people taught mental health and balance.

Once more I was discovering that what I read in the books would stay like a picture in my mind. I started acing all the tests, and ever since then, through the years I took college classes off and on, I always maintained a four point average. I myself don't know how it has happened. Others may take it lightly, but it was an amazing thing to me. I can only give credit to the Creator for his gifts, for being with me through my life.

With the education I had, I went on to become a substance abuse counselor, and two years ago I became internationally certified. I eventually took the best of my people's teachings of how to walk in balance and the things I had learned of psychology and brought them to my counseling, and it was marvelous to see how people of all races could relate to these teachings.

Even while I was in college, I would answer the call to go wherever I was needed by AIM and my people. We Indians will travel many miles to go to the funeral of a friend or relation, so that was my excuse whenever I had to get away. My professors must have wondered why so many of my people were passing on. When I had to return to college, I'd get a lot of kidding from my partners in AIM; they said I must have found some rich white lady to take me in. I'd say, "No, man, I'm going to school," and they knew why. They knew that, along with being strong in our own ways, we would have to have many that were educated in the white man's world to help stand up for our people. Sometimes when I go to the reservations I hear young people say the reason they drink is that there's nothing to do on the rez. I tell them to sober up, and then they'll see that there's a heck of a lot to be done. They could get their education in spite of all the pressures against them and one day be able to help their people. The Great Spirit had given me a gift, and there are gifts he gives to each of us. But to find that gift I had to take that first step to help myself. We can ask for things and pray for things, but we have to meet the Great Spirit halfway. This is what I would tell the young people coming up— that there are many gifts the Creator gives to each of us, but we have to find them and nourish and understand them, or they will be wasted.

Louis's great-great grandfather and namesake, Two Ravens.

Louis's father, Louis Irwin, Sr. (Two Men).

Louis with his parents.

Louis going into the Army;
he was 17 years old
when he went to Korea.

Louis as a baby.

*Louis with hatchet and pistol on the Longest Walk.*

*Louis with his fist raised at the Big Mountain, Arizona, protest in 1986.*

*March at Big Mountain. Note the upside-down flag—the international signal of distress.*

*Archie Fire Lame Deer building the sweat lodge on Louis and Daphne's land in the Ozarks.*

*Joe Chasing Horse, Leonard Peltier, Louis, and Arvol Looking Horse, keeper of the Sacred Calf Pipe, at Leavenworth.*

*Steve Roubidou, Louis, and Russell Means.*

*Leonard Peltier and Louis at powwow sponsored by Leavenworth prisoners.*

*Leonard Peltier Day in Washington, D.C., the year before Louis passed on. Below, Louis addresses the rally.*

*Louis was a wonderful storyteller. (photographs by Ron Martin.)*

*Above, Louis with his wife Daphne. (photograph by Sam Lines.) Right, Louis and his son John. Below, Louis with his brother Kenny and their father.*

# 9

# BENEATH THE SACRED TREE

Although I felt the Great Spirit's presence throughout my life, I didn't truly begin my spiritual walk until I set foot on the sacred Sun Dance grounds. It is there that I found the truth and meaning of the teachings that had always been within me—the teachings of my grandfather and the Old Ones about the natural life and laws of the Creator and the Earth, and of walking in balance. It was a time when the men and women in AIM were seeking out the elders to relearn their culture and their spiritual ways. At the same time, AIM had given the elders the courage to bring the old ceremonies out in the open again.

A lot of AIM members were from the cities and had had little exposure to their own culture. But I had seen the old ceremonies and remember the time when my people still had our chiefs. Sometimes I think some of us Native American people don't appreciate what we were born into or given, things that white people are hungry for. What I had seen and been through in the white man's world made me question the worth of those teachings, even though I knew they were good and true. I had been to many of our ceremonies, and I knew that many people were healed through them, but only when I turned my life over to Tunkashila, when I quit trying to be the controller, did I become something besides a drunk who wallowed around in self-pity and thought only of himself.

Many old prophecies were fulfilled when the Sun Dance was brought out into the open again. Long ago my Mandan people had the Okeepa ceremony, which is recognized as the "mother" of the Sun Dance. The Hidatsas practiced the Sun Dance, and I remember being taken to the Sun Dance at my home when I was young. But it was very secret in those days, and my people had to hold them way back in the Badlands because the government had outlawed it as a barbaric ritual. In fact, laws passed in the 1890s had forbidden the Indian people the right to practice even the simplest ceremonies. It seemed almost impossible to believe when I was young, but the prophecies spoke of how the Sun Dance would come back into the open once more and be stronger than ever.

Through the Sun Dance our most sacred ceremonies and instruments of worship are brought together. Those who have pledged to dance are cleansed in the sacred Lodge of Purification, and they bring their pipes into the sacred Sun Dance circle, where they dance for four days without food or water. The Sun Dance circle represents the universe, and in the middle of the circle is placed the cottonwood tree that is the Tree of Life, reaching from the earth to the heavens. It is also the tree of our ancestors and the seed of those yet unborn, and the prayers of the people are placed as offerings in its branches. Through the tree our prayers are directed to the Great Spirit, and the Spirit descends through the tree, through the dancers, and out to the people under the arbor, who are also a part of the circle, and flows out as a blessing for all things. We also know that our ancestors dance with us there.

And so the dancers dance as a sacrifice, as a prayer for their people, for all nations, and for all living things. The Sun Dance is held in the summer, when life is at its fullest, when the animals have their young and the berries are ripe, and the Sun Dance is also a dance of thanksgiving for the many gifts of the Earth and a prayer for the growth and life of all living things. Many of the male dancers are pierced during the dance and tied to the Sacred Tree; others are pierced and drag the buffalo skulls. The piercing is not a test of bravery or some kind of initiation. Those who vow to pierce do so because of a powerful dream or vision, or take it on as a vow for a sick relative. In this way we make a small sacrifice of the only thing we can offer our Creator, our flesh. We can't offer the Creator money or cars or a fancy church; all these things he owns already. The Christians worship a man who made a great sacrifice for them; in our ways there is no one who can do that for us. There are those who say the little bit of pain men offer in the piercing is to remind us of the great pain that women go through in giving birth.

Those who have danced the Sun Dance for four years must then go on to carry the pipe for the people. They dedicate their lives to working for the people and to walking in balance. The pipe is our holiest instrument of worship, something the Creator gave us that we can see and feel and hold on to. We do not pray to the pipe, but we pray through it; it is our connection to the Creator, and we try to live by what it represents. The pipe is the two joined as one; it is an altar. When we fill the pipe, we place all things in the universe in there, and with it we join our breath with the breath of all living things and send it as a prayer to the Great Spirit and the powers of the universe. The pipe represents the *chunka luta*, the good Red Road, the way of walking in balance with the Earth and with all our relations, and so it represents Truth. Only the truth and good thoughts must be kept while smoking the *chanupa*, the Sacred Pipe; and so it represents peace and understanding between peoples.

Those who carry the pipe are not perfect; they're just people with problems like everybody else. But they have made a commitment to walk the Red Road, to do their best to dedicate their lives to seeking balance and working for the good of the people. Whether or not we have the physical pipe with us, we must still walk this road, for we ourselves become the pipe.

Among the Lakotas it was a woman, White Buffalo Calf Woman, who brought the Sacred Pipe to the People, and it was she who taught the ways of the Red Road. The Lakotas still keep the pipe that she brought; it is very ancient and is made from the leg bone of a buffalo calf. This pipe represents the life that Tunkashila gives to the People and to all of creation, and it reminds us that nothing that is made by man is as holy as that which is made by the Creator.

Not all those that have a pipe are pipe carriers. There are personal pipes and pipes that people hold for their family. Actually, anyone can possess a pipe; it is just a piece of rock and wood. But what it represents is sacred, and there is no end to what can be learned from the pipe. It is not something to be taken lightly. You can't just go buy a ceremonial pipe and start fooling around with it; you could hurt yourself and others. Prayers can be answered through the pipe, but you have to be careful what you ask for. There are reasons why we do things by steps; this is hard to understand for some white people who want all the knowledge before there is the understanding.

The pipe can be the heaviest thing in the world to carry. There were many times when I felt I wasn't worthy to carry the pipe, and many times I fell away. My spiritual awakening came slowly. I gradually learned how to live a clean life, a life free from alcohol and drugs and jealousy and hate. I learned how to live that life for my Creator.

There is no end to that learning, and I still have a long way to go.

╾╼

Back in the late 1960s, the Lakota Sun Dance was held in the open for the first time in this century. Even though some of the dancers were serious about what they were doing, the tribal council was promoting it as a tourist attraction. They had hot dog stands and everything. No piercing was allowed. When the Lakota traditionals began to find their voice again, with the help of AIM, there began to be more and more Sun Dances. But now they were being held back in the hills, and the traditional ceremony was brought back.

One of the places that the Sun Dance was brought back was at Crow Dog's Paradise, a piece of land with woods and a pretty creek that belonged to Henry Crow Dog and his family on the Rosebud Reservation in South Dakota. Henry had brought his family there years before, in the 1930s, when he was driven out of Saint Francis, South Dakota, during a blizzard by the missionaries for practicing traditional ceremonies. Their family from way back was made up of warriors and keepers of the traditional Lakota ways through all those years when the government had forbidden the Indian people to practice their way of worship. The old man Henry was a very wise man, and he led a simple life there. Many times I would sit and talk with Henry. His son Leonard was brought up with all the ceremonies and was a young spiritual leader who stood behind AIM even when many of the medicine men wouldn't. Leonard was one of the strongest ones at Wounded Knee. He also paid the price for standing up for his people; he was harassed by the FBI, his home was raided, and his family beaten. He spent over a year and a half in a maximum security prison.

Already there were people from my home who had come south to the Lakotas to relearn the Sun Dance because the elders saw that our *tihanshes,* our Lakota cousins, had kept it alive and were bringing it into the open once again. My uncle Carl Whitman had adopted Leonard Crow Dog into his family; this is how we make relations in our ways. The one thing that the white man did do for us is to bring even more unity to the Indian people, especially between nations that often warred on each other. It was an exciting time when Indian people everywhere were waking up to their power and sharing their sacred ways.

For four years I was the fire man at the Sun Dance at Crow Dog's, carrying rocks for the sun dancers, who go into the Purification Lodge every morning before dawn and again in the evening. The fire man should know the importance of what he does, because the fire and the rocks he handles are sacred. That fire represents the life that is passed on from generation to generation. There's a lot to be learned from the hard work of being fire man, and at the time I didn't think I could be a sun dancer; I didn't see how I could ever dedicate my life to the People when I couldn't even manage my own life.

It was the second day of Sun Dance one year, late at night, and I was standing by the fire. Carl Whitman, who was the Okeepa chief of my people, was standing over in the shadows there. Before the Garrison Dam was built, Carl was one who really pushed the white man's way, but after they flooded our homes he returned to our traditional ways, tried to bring back some of our old ceremonies. He was also a professor with many degrees. Carl and I started talking.

"There's only a few of us Mandan-Hidatsas out there dancing," Carl said.

"I don't want to go out there," I said. "I can work and help out here, and I can eat well and drink. I'm better off here, working at the fire."

"Oh no, I'm not telling you to dance; nobody can tell you to do that. But we are here."

The next day, without hardly knowing why, I was out under the Sacred Tree to make a pledge to dance the next year. Grandpa Henry Crow Dog and Leonard Crow Dog were at the tree with me. "I don't know what I'm doing here," I said.

"Ah, nobody knows," Grandpa Henry said. "Maybe there's something you can do for your people—their drinking, your drinking, all these things. Someday, though, you will see. Something will be given to you, and someday you will do good things for your people."

That night they told me I wouldn't be carrying the rocks. I was supposed to go stay out under the Sun Dance arbor. It was nighttime, and I made myself comfortable facing the Sacred Tree over by where they drum. I looked at the tree, and I looked at it and looked at it. Late that night I fell asleep, and in a dream I saw my people dancing, dancing. It was the Okeepa, and my people were all coming out of their houses and lodges and going into the big lodge. They were my relatives, my fathers, my grandfathers and grandmothers and long-ago ancestors. There were even ones from the present day that I didn't know at that time; I would get to know them later and realize that they had been in my dream. They were my people dancing. In our ways I knew that somehow I had to finish that dream.

The next year I was traveling around with some of my AIM buddies, and we arrived at Crow Dog's Paradise just before the start of Sun Dance. I still didn't have any real intention of dancing. I had no pipe, no Sun Dance skirt; the only eagle feather I owned was the one given to me after I went out into the Badlands, and my father kept that one. But Grandpa Henry called me over and presented me with a pipe. My Lakota aunties made me a Sun Dance skirt and a sage crown. Everything I needed was given to me. I felt very humble, and now there was no backing out of my commitment.

Leonard Crow Dog gave us a talk, as he usually does the night before the Sun Dance begins. He asked us why we wanted to sun dance. "Do you want to look important out there? Do you want to catch the eye of some good-looking girl under the arbor? Are you trying to be tough? Are you trying to gain powers or something? When you dance, you should be out there for Tunkashila and for your people. You think about why you're out there." I had many doubts myself, but there I was the next morning, with no eagle feathers, way at the back of the line with the children, and I was honored.

Every year since then I have danced at Crow Dog's. The songs and the drum and the prayers are all beautiful. I always dance hard; I try to dance for the glory of God. After a time I discovered how to "get inside" the drum, to make the drum and myself and the heartbeat of the earth one. It seems like when I "get inside" the drum I could dance forever. That drum will never leave you. You will know balance when the drum inside you and the drum outside, the world outside you, beat as one.

Over the years that I have danced I always knew that there was something that held me up when I knew I had no more strength. Sometimes I was even given a spiritual "drink of water" when I thought I would die from the thirst. On the last day of the dance there is a healing round, where the people are brought out from the arbor and into the Sun Dance circle, where they can receive healings from the Sacred Tree and from the dancers, who go down the line of people, blessing them and praying for them, for they are given a sacred power through their dancing. One year, before the healing round, Archie Fire Lame Deer came around to the dancers, pouring a gourdful of cool water in front of our faces. This is to remind us of why we are out there dancing, and of just how sacred water is, the Water of Life. Archie poured the water in front of me, and I fanned him with my eagle-wing fan, giving him a little cool breeze. Right then I felt my mouth fill with water. Things like this are hard for non-Indians to understand, but this is how we help each other.

There was one year that the Lakotas were trying to bring back the pulling of buffalo skulls. In this way of sacrificing, a dancer is pierced in his back and attached to a line of buffalo skulls, which he must drag around the Sacred Circle four times, stopping to pray at each of the Four Directions. Some of the skulls weigh twenty-five pounds or more; even so, it is not easy to break free, and sometimes they'll have children sit on the skulls so the dancer can break free.

They were trying to bring the pulling of the skulls back, but the young men were having a really hard time. This way of sacrifice was originally a part of the Okeepa ceremony of my Mandan people; my people were the original buffalo hunters of the Great Plains and keepers of the buffalo ceremonies. Maybe that is why Archie called me over and said that I should try to pull the skulls and help out the young men. I was hooked up to the skulls and immediately knew that the buffalo were with me. They were right there all around me. I could smell them, I could feel their hot breath on me, I could hear their grunts, I could almost touch them as I made my way around the Sun Dance circle four times. After the four rounds they were going to pull me off the skulls, but I motioned them away. I stood up and held my staff in front of me. I raised my hands, and as I prayed, the ropes flew off my back. It was the spirits that had released me.

Many people do not understand why we still use the buffalo in our ceremonies. There is a rawhide buffalo that is made to hang in the Sacred Tree. The buffalo skull is used on the altar, for a part of the spirit of the buffalo remains in the skull as long as the horns are attached.

The buffalo is honored, not only because it fed us and clothed us and gave us shelter or because of our past glory, but also because the Indian and the buffalo still share the same fate. We were both penned up on little reservations, so we're like a curiosity now. But the buffalo also represents the future. The prophecy of the Ghost Dance and many other prophecies say that the buffalo will return at a time when the whole earth is going to be renewed and the Indian people will become strong again. We can see that the prophecy is already coming true, for now there are buffalo all over the country, and the spirit of the natives of this land is returning. The spirit of the buffalo likes to see the People have plenty and be happy and get along. The buffalo spirit helps those that are generous and work hard for the People.

I have seen many lives turned around through the Sun Dance. One year a few Native American prisoners in South Dakota were given permission to take part in the Sun Dance at Crow Dog's, and I volunteered to drive my Thunderbird to pick them up. I was a little nervous, but things went smoothly, and when we got there the people were all lined up to honor them. These were men who had been in and out of prisons their whole lives, men who were addicted to drugs and alcohol, and I can say that every one of them went on to get out of prison and live a clean life and follow these ways. One year a prisoner took off, and that put an end to the prisoner release program; but much good came of it, and it should be started up again.

Many good people and many teachers I have met through the Sun Dance. At Crow Dog's Paradise I was adopted by Ednah New Rider Weber. I call her Mama because she has been just like a mother to me, and I have always tried to be a good son to her. We first met at the Sun Dance at Big Mountain. Ednah is Pawnee, and the Pawnee are closely related to my mother's Arickara people.

I invited Ednah and her daughter Ramona, who became my adopted sister, to Crow Dog's. I used to tell Ramona that there was a little Indian inside her that wanted to come out, a little Indian that wanted to dance. Ednah was shocked when Ramona came into the Sun Dance circle. She has been a strong dancer at Crow Dog's ever since.

There were many things I witnessed within the Sun Dance circle, many visions and healings, things the dominant culture would call miracles. Every year there are men and women dancing who shouldn't physically be able to be out there, but they dance with the power that flows through the Sacred Tree. For us, miracles are not something that happened thousands of years ago; we see each moment as a miracle of the Creator, the same Creator now as thousands of years ago. Also, we don't have a word for "supernatural"; everything for us is natural, the natural laws of the Creator. The laws of the spirit world are different from the laws of the world we see, however; that is why we call it the Great Mystery. I have seen many physical healings and the healing of lives. When I dance I carry a hoop, and in it is a web of sinew that represents the Great Weaver, the one who weaves our life and our dreams and our fate together, and through it I have seen healings that will take place, and through it I have seen visions in the sun.

For four years I danced with the pipe that was held for me by Grandpa Henry. When the dance was over I would return the pipe to him. After the fourth year Henry held his hands up when it was time to return the pipe. "You keep this pipe," he said, "Now you must carry this pipe for the People." I felt pitiful, that of all people I should be honored with the Sacred Pipe, and I cried. I cherished that pipe, even though I felt unworthy to carry it, and I hardly ever brought it out.

When I began in the Sun Dance I was dancing for my Indian people: for all the struggles they were involved in, and for all the things that AIM was fighting for. I was still a militant, and carried a lot of anger toward the white man's government. One year I even had the pipe taken from me. We were having a sacred sweat, and I was in one of my more militant moods. I gathered up all the guns that were around and laid them on the sacred Purification Lodge as if they were going to be blessed. After that sweat Archie Fire Lame Deer called me over to his tent and asked for my pipe. He kept it all that year.

Let me tell you that it is easy to sun dance. Maybe it's not the easiest thing to dance four days out in the blazing sun with no food or water, but people can do it with sheer physical strength. There are even some that go from Sun Dance to Sun Dance. But taking part in the ceremony is the easy part. What is hard is to stay within that Sacred Circle, to stay within the balance through the rest of the year, within our daily lives. That is the hard part. Spirituality is not just dancing the Sun Dance, it is not having a pipe and calling oneself a pipe carrier, it's not seeing and hearing mysterious things in the sacred Purification Lodge. Spirituality is doing our best to walk the walk, and to walk our talk, every day that is given to us by our Creator.

Even when I began to sun dance every year, I would still fall away from my spiritual walk. For many years I would do really well for half a year or more, and then for one reason or another I would take that first drink and it would go downhill from there. But through the Sun Dance I was given hope. It helped me to see that there was a purpose in our lives. The more I went to the Sun Dance and into the Lodge of Purification, the more my life began to change.

# 10

# THE BLACKMOUTH

In my dream under the Sacred Tree I had seen my people dancing, and more and more were coming into the sacred lodge. It was like a seed of the Tree of Life that had been buried for many years and was now sprouting and coming into the light of day. My Mandan, Hidatsa, and Arickara people had never completely forgotten their spiritual ways; they had kept them in their hearts. But they had suffered such defeat at the hands of the white man that many felt that the Old Ways had no place in the white man's world they had been thrown into.

The Three Tribes had been out on the plains for a long, long time before the Lakota and Cheyenne and others ever wandered out there. My people built big fortified villages, and their warriors were respected everywhere. They were wealthy in the things the land provided for them. They were great traders, and the white man came to their villages because of the friendliness of the people. Yet it all nearly ended when smallpox was brought by the white man. Hundreds and hundreds of my people died, and their grief went on and on. At the same time, they were beginning to see the treachery and greed of the white man, his broken promises.

Four Bears was the famous chief of the Mandan. In all the history books he is portrayed as the one who befriended Lewis and Clark, the signer of treaties and the great friend of the white man. There are famous paintings of Four Bears. Four Bears was also honored by the People as a great and generous chief, and as a great warrior who bore many scars from battles in defense of his people and from his sacrifices in the sacred Okeepa ceremony. He was a great warrior, but he couldn't fight this thing that was destroying the People. As he lay there dying and scarred from the smallpox, he called the People to his side and told them, "Look what they have done to me. Now even the wolves turn their heads when they see my face. I, Four Bears, gave them safety. I was the one who befriended them and called them my brothers. Beware of these people! They will not be satisfied until they have taken our land and destroyed us completely. Go, now, you must go and kill every one of them, every man, woman, and child!" Those were the last, desperate words of Four Bears, and you won't read them in any history book.

That isn't what the People did. Yet some still follow those words—not literally, but there are those who feel that they must separate themselves from the white man and his ways of treachery and his disease of greed, and that they must keep their ceremonies separate from the white man. They say that the white man will always be a mouse—he can only see what is in front of him, not what is beyond. When he looks beyond, he sees only what is for himself, and when he sees that, he'll look a little further and see more for himself. We must pray for these people, they say, for you'll see how they treat each other and kill each other right and left, and finally you will see how they treat the Earth, our Mother.

They didn't follow the words of Four Bears, but after the smallpox our warriors were busy, as the Lakotas and other tribes tried to plunder my people's villages in our weakened condition. The few warriors we had held them off. Many times in the past, four or five of our great warriors would face many enemies. They were taught that if they and the people believed in their medicine, they could do anything, against great odds. It was the Blackmouth, a society of warriors founded long ago, who were given the duty to protect the People. These were the original Dog Soldiers, the ones who would plant the lance and could not retreat from the enemy; only a fellow Blackmouth could release them. Without them our enemies might have finished us off. The Blackmouths were also like the policemen of the tribe, and their society finally died out when the tribal police came along and took over many of their duties.

Eventually the Mandan and Hidatsa, who had always been close, joined with the Arickara in one village: three tribes that would always stand together. But the huge tract of land they fought so hard to defend, land that was solemnly promised to us as a nation by the Fort Laramie Treaty, was taken away and carved up over and over, until we were left with only a little reservation. Then laws were passed forbidding us to practice our religion and our way of life. Many of my people became Christians. Finally, a dam covered our homes and farms with a lake. Now there is too much alcohol, too much suicide, too many people who have to live on handouts. When I was young we still had our unity, our chiefs, our own ways of governing, and we were an almost totally self-sufficient people.

Even as our culture was being taken from us, some of my people maintained the sacred bundles and kept the stories and the Old Ways in their hearts. When our Lakota cousins brought the Sun Dance back out into the open, it gave us the courage to reclaim our spiritual ways. Today our languages are being taught in the schools, and there is much more interest in our sacred bundles and clan histories. Some have also had the visions to bring back our sacred Okeepa ceremony, the mother of the Sun Dance. Some of the rites of the Okeepa have been held, but we await the visions to carry out other parts. There are parts that were left out because of those who felt they might offend someone. One of the Okeepa dancers is called the Foolish One, and he has no respect for sacred things. The Foolish One carries with him a large penis; there is a reason for this and lessons in it about power that is used in foolish ways. There are those who feel that the Foolish One is indecent, and those who feel that the full power of the ceremony will not return to the people if things are left out.

My people still have their shrines and their sacred places. One still looks after the Lone Man shrine, which used to be set up in the middle of the Mandan villages. It is a standing hoop made of wood to represent the enclosure Lone Man made to save our people from the great flood. We have kept three of the turtle drums. These drums are important and ancient ceremonial objects of the Mandan, and they come into this story. They are said to be actual sea turtles that came to the Mandan people and offered themselves to be used as drums when the people come together in ceremony. The turtles stand for strength and long life, and they also represent this land we walk on. It is said that the drums can even turn themselves back into turtles. They say that originally there were four drums, but that one of them was unhappy with the people and turned back into a turtle and disappeared into the water. There are old prophecies that say that when the people are once again living in a good way, when they come back within the Sacred Hoop, the fourth turtle will return.

So the old ways of ceremony were returning to my home up north. I began to feel that I must return there to find out something about myself, something connected to the teachings of my own Mandan, Hidatsa, and Arickara people. In 1983 I moved back to North Dakota to further my education in alcohol and drug counseling at the University of North Dakota at Minot.

Over the years I had traveled back to Fort Berthold many times. Many people there thought of me as a crazy militant, but I had always made it a point to visit the elders and bring them a little something, and I listened carefully to their words and stories. Now when I returned, I began to take part in the sweat lodges and ceremonies that were being held by a small group of my people who were trying to bring back our traditional ways. I spoke to some of the elders about feeling that I had returned to my people for a spiritual purpose. They told me that I should be put out on a fast to talk to my Creator and maybe find the answers I was looking for.

Two of those that were keeping the old ways alive at my home were the old man Ralph and his nephew Sammy. Ralph has since passed away, but his nephew continues on as a medicine man among our people. And so I came to Ralph and Sammy and asked them to take me out on the hill. This is something that is done with ceremony and preparation. You must approach the medicine person with a pipe and offerings; and if they are accepted they will tell you how to prepare. I was told to make prayer ties of tobacco wrapped in strips of cloth of the sacred colors. These are offerings for the spirits that are made with prayers. Your loved ones can also help you make these ties, so their prayers will also be with you out on the hill.

After the sweat lodge ceremony you are taken out with your prayer ties; the ties are wrapped around four chokecherry branches placed at the Four Directions. You are dressed only in moccasins and a breechcloth, and you carry only a pipe, with which you will pray to your Creator. Among my people food and water is sometimes brought along as an offering for the spirits. The food is corn balls, meat, squash, and berries. Some people might say that this a great temptation for someone who will be out for four days without food or water, but that offering is for the spirits, and there is no fooling the spirits.

We lay sage down in the sacred area where we fast, and when you enter that space it's just you and the Creator out there. Of course, you're out there with all your fears and problems. Every thought and emotion comes to you: loneliness and boredom and everything you've said and done, good and bad. We are pitiful out there, we feel like the smallest creature, but because we are pitiful we begin to pray. We are taught that prayer is a two-way conversation, and we must also listen—not just with our ears, but with our hearts and our whole being. We're not out there to seek glorious visions or great powers, we're there to pray for our lives, to pray that we can do something good for the people, to find out how we can come into balance, to pray to our Creator. We can't impress the spirits with the things we have or how great we are, but they come close when they hear prayers that are sincere, and they can teach many things. We give up our little self, so that we can hear the voice of the Great Spirit within us and around us.

So there I was high up on a butte overlooking the waters that covered our once-beautiful valley. It was summertime in North Dakota, when the days are very long. Among my people we usually stand facing west when we pray, during the fast, for that is the direction from where the spirits come. When we can no longer stand we can lie down, and sometimes we have strong dreams.

The People knew I was up there, and I stood praying, praying, praying. At night there were strange noises. I heard sounds like people under the earth, and they were talking and sounded like they were moving big objects around underground. I tried to remember what they said about the spirits coming: there are spirits that will tempt you or try to frighten you, but you must hold fast to the pipe.

There are those who have even seen headlights where there is no road, and a car full of drunks will pull up and offer them a drink. These are spirits coming to tempt us. Sometimes our worst fears and worries come from our own minds, and we may even see them, or we may see people from our past or people far away. But only the good spirits can enter the Sacred Circle.

At night a person feels very small and alone. I began to hear a *tchkk, tchkk, tchkk,* a loud rattling behind me, and I thought there were rattlesnakes around. I prayed hard that they would respect the Sacred Circle. I told that rattlesnake that if he bit me I'd see him on the other side and we'd have it out.

During the day the mosquitoes were almost unbearable, as they usually are at that time of year, and they made it very hard to pray. On the second day a marvelous thing happened. The mosquitoes were almost eating me alive, but all of a sudden I could see a huge cloud of dragonflies come out of nowhere and swarm all around me. Those dragonflies ate up all the mosquitoes and then flew away. It was a real blessing. Early the next morning there came a herd of wild horses, and their leader was a big white stallion. He came very close to my circle and reared up and showed me his beauty and his strength.

Just as when I was young and went out into the Badlands, I began to feel a part of the circle of the sun and the moon and the stars as they traveled above my own little circle. I truly began to feel the power of the Creator all around me. Then another funny thing happened. Across the way from where I stood I saw a bunch of people that I recognized walking to a spot on a hillside where they were going to have a picnic. These were people that knew I was fasting there. They were wolfing down hamburgers and drinking cold pop; it made me awfully hungry and thirsty. Then it came to me: "That's OK," I thought. "I could have what you have, but you can't have what I have now." Just then a big whirlwind kicked up. That wind came and blew those people's picnic away. Their stuff was flying everywhere, and they practically ran out of there.

On the third morning my mouth was dry as dust and I was feeling weak. This whole time I was standing on a hill and looking out over a whole lake of water. I could no longer stand, and I prayed. I said, "I am thirsty, I am sick," and then suddenly I felt my mouth fill with water. I felt strong again, and I knew I would make it through. I stood up again, and as I looked out over the waters of the lake I could see a large object floating out there. I thought it was a boat, but then I could see it was a huge turtle swimming. I could see the waves he was making in the water. The turtle was swimming to the other shore, but then he turned toward me, and I could feel his words inside me. He told me that he had been gone a long time, but things were not good with the People; he was angry. He wouldn't return until my people settled things out here. He said that he was in the Missouri River, and that the river was still there, still under the waters; that one day the river would return. Then the turtle dived under the water and was gone.

That night Sammy and a few others came to pray with me. No one is supposed to look at the faster, and they were facing away from me. We were singing prayer songs, and whenever we'd start singing you could hear the coyotes start their singing, like they were answering back. Sammy said those were old-time warriors and they were happy.

The morning of the fifth day there was a group that came to take me down. When they come for the faster they aren't supposed to look at them, but as the helpers came up the hill, some of them looked my way and saw a bear where I was standing, and a man dressed and painted in the old way passing in front of my altar and disappearing into the bushes.

We were starting to leave when I looked down and saw a little weed that rattled in the wind; this was the rattlesnake noise. I knew in my heart that this was a medicine, and I made an offering and took some of the seed pods. I will keep them until I know more about the medicine. Out of my fear came something good.

When we returned there were a lot of my people gathered there; some had come for healing. We went into the sweat lodge, where I told about the turtle and the things I had seen and heard, and the people were happy. After the purification Ralph took me to the side and gave me a small bundle all wrapped up. Ralph told me that he had had a dream that told him to make up the bundle, and that one was coming who was to receive it. "You keep this bundle," he said. "We'll see what happens. For now you keep it with you, but don't ever open the bundle."

I kept that bundle with my medicine things, and of course I was curious to know what was in it. Other times, though, I almost forgot I had it. I think that the old man Ralph knew that although I had fasted and received some things in vision, I still was not ready to live up to my spiritual commitments. A spiritual gift is only a seed that must be watered and taken care of to grow into something of benefit to the People.

I was feeling very strong after my fast. Soon after, I got a position working as an alcohol and drug counselor at Fort Berthold and started up a program that I knew was going to help my people. Under this program the people that would normally be hauled off to sit in jail for alcohol-related problems could instead find help for their disease through counseling or be sent into treatment. I felt good about the work I was doing, in spite of all the red tape and politics of dealing with tribal government.

But after a while the people that came for counseling really started to trouble me. I knew firsthand why they drank; I might even be able to help the person that came to me, but I could do nothing about the causes. All around me I witnessed the racism of the white store owners and ranchers who leased our land and treated my people like dirt—and on our own land! I knew the lack of self-esteem, the history of broken families, and the alcohol and despair. Finally, I sought help myself. Then I broke down; instead of facing the problem, I skipped out and went on a big binge. I became a crazy man once again. I went into treatment, but I didn't finish. I tried to return to work, but they had fired me from my job.

⚞

I had begun my spiritual walk, yet I was still trying to make it on my own. I hadn't turned my life over to Tunkashila. I thought I could do good things, like my fast, and still keep my anger and resentments inside where no one would know about them. But they still ate away inside me. Then my old alcoholic behaviors would come out. When things were going well, I'd find a way to sabotage them; when things got rough, I'd just run away. Then, somehow, I'd wind up taking that first drink. It seems that we always turn to our bottle or our pills or our closetful of excuses before we'll admit we're not in control and before we'll honor our commitments.

Soon after I was fired from my job, I landed in jail in Pine Ridge, and the cops smashed up my Thunderbird. That car has been with me all over the country, and it's still my baby. When they let me out I went on a big drunk and wallowed around in my anger and self-pity. Some friends said I should go stay with Billy Good Voice Elk for a while, that maybe he could help me get myself together. Billy had always supported the people in AIM who came to help in the struggles of the traditional Lakotas, even though many of the medicine people refused to have anything to do with the "outsiders" in AIM. He was a heyoka medicine man, one who worked with the powers of the Thunder Beings. Through his life he gained knowledge of many medicine ways and ceremonies of his people and could use them in his doctoring, according to what a person needed. These ways are something like different methods of psychotherapy and are used for mental, emotional, spiritual, and physical healing. He was also a good man, one of the true old-timers, who lived in a very humble way and was always giving everything he had away to his people.

Billy taught me many things but never asked why I was there. He knew why I was there. He was going to put me through a traditional "detox" program. Every day we got up at dawn to pray and worked hard all day cutting wood and doing other jobs, and every day we would have a sweat. After a while my mind was clearer, and every day I got stronger. Billy taught me that we work at our spirituality day by day. We may not feel worthy; we may not feel like our prayers are being heard or that we can do any good for anybody. We may not even feel worthy enough to pray before the Great Spirit. But instead of praying for this or that, we can just pray for strength to meet the day ahead. Each day we pray and we do the work, and the work becomes our spirituality. The work *is* our spirituality. Our daily walk is our spiritual path. This is how we try to stay within the Sun Dance circle. We try to live each day in gratitude to our Creator. We do not try for perfection; we just try to get a little closer to being in balance within ourselves and in balance with the Creation.

After my stay with Billy Good Voice Elk, I knew I had to turn my life over to a higher power. I knew I had to face my greatest enemy, the one within me. That is a hard thing to do. After my stay with Billy, in 1985, I fell off the wagon once more, and it would be the last time. But I fell off big-time; I nearly drank myself to death.

I was in Minneapolis and had been on a month-long binge. I took a bus to Kansas City, and by the time I got there I was going through the d.t.'s. There was a cop there, a man I will always be grateful to. He could see what kind of shape I was in, and he bought me a beer on the way to a treatment center. I wound up at the VA hospital in Kansas City. For a while I was hooked up to all kinds of tubes and machines, just to keep me alive. After they got me through that I went into a treatment program, but nobody there had much hope that I would ever be cured. My psychologist was interested in Indian alcohol issues, and we would talk about how my people could be helped. As part of my treatment she had me go to the little town of White Clay, Nebraska, to take notes on what I saw there. The town is just over the state line from the Pine Ridge Reservation. It's a place where Lakotas drift in from morning to night to beg, borrow, or steal for liquor. I sat there and I watched the people stumble in and out of the liquor stores all day. I was still close in time to being one of them, and I knew their anger and hopelessness. I felt a lot of guilt because I was sitting there in a nice car with a few traveler's checks in my pocket. That is a hard thing to do for most Indian people, for in our ways you give whatever you have to a relation who is in need. But I knew I couldn't drink with them; I couldn't go joyriding and smash up my car, something that happened almost every day on that stretch of highway they call "Deadman's Alley." My money would only go for more liquor. I felt helpless as I watched the power of the mighty Lakota nation being pissed away with a bottle of wine.

After I had sat on that street corner in White Clay I knew that the only thing that would help the Indian people with this disease of alcohol was to return to our own spiritual ways, back to the Red Road. This was the only way that we could end the cycles of despair, the cycles of alcoholism and broken families and low self-esteem that were now being passed down through generations. At the same time, alcoholism is a white man's disease; many of my people's problems come from living within the dominant culture, and most of us battling alcohol will have to go into the white man's treatment before we can deal with some of those issues and be strong in our own beliefs. But I began to see a way to bridge both ways, combining the best of the white man's psychology and counseling with the best of the psychology and spirituality of my people.

After my experience in White Clay I never took another drink. I know I owe my life to the teachings of the Red Road. Soon after, I began to use my grandfather's and my elders' teachings and the ways of the Red Road in my counseling. For Indian people I showed them the Sacred Circle we are born into and walk in this life, and how to begin to find balance as we walk. Sometimes Indian people have trouble with the white man's concept of God, and they can't relate to some of the teachings of AA as easily as they can to the spirituality of their own cultures.

The basic teachings I was given are universal. With those of other races I didn't use words like Red Road, or speak of the Purification Lodge or the Sacred Tree, but I used those same teachings in a different language, and it was wonderful to see how people of all races and walks of life used them to change their lives. People with much more schooling than I had started coming around and wanting to observe my methods. Of course, it had nothing to do with me; it was the teachings of the natural laws, the natural ways of the Creator, teachings that have been permanent for thousands of years.

⇌

I had fought a lot of battles within myself and with others, but the only way I was truly able to win was when I surrendered. The only way I was able to turn my own life around was by turning my life over to Tunkashila. It wasn't hard for me to believe in a power greater than myself; I had believed in the Great Spirit Chief, my Creator, ever since I was old enough to understand. I saw his miracles in the land and sky. I had witnessed Tunkashila's miracles and healings in the Sun Dance, the Purification Lodge, the fast, the pipe ceremonies. I knew Tunkashila had saved my life many times. I had no trouble with faith in a higher power, but I felt I had to hang on to that little bit of control, to that place inside me that kept the little secrets, the little fears, the anger, the things I thought were me.

Many of us can fall into that trap: "As long as I go to church or the sweat lodge, as long as I put an offering in the plate, as long as I try to take care of my life according to society, I'll be OK." We think we can keep those little resentments and fears and no one will know. Others thought I was strong and doing good things, but in my heart, I was out of balance. The drum within me did not beat to the drum of the world around me. We know this in our hearts to be true, yet we convince ourselves that we have to carry those things around and they eat us away inside. We cannot fool Tunkashila, though. The Great Spirit knows our hearts, the deepest things within us, and so we begin to pray from the heart, and what comes from the heart reaches the heart. Then we begin to turn our lives over to the Great Spirit; we let its power into our lives. We have a God-given conscience, a higher power within us that communicates with God, that knows right from wrong. We begin to listen to our higher power, and then every day we try, not for perfection, but to stay in balance and to maintain that conscious contact with God. That is when we truly begin our spiritual walk.

"Spiritual awakening" didn't happen in a flash for me. It meant gradually coming to know and feel the changes that were happening within me. It meant slowly developing a clean and clear mind. It meant suddenly being able to smile at someone I had thought was my enemy. I used to think about my enemies out there, but I began to know that I was my own worst enemy. I was beginning to look at the anger that drove my militancy and violence, and I made a commitment instead to try to take a positive role in change. I learned that it is only when we can pray for our enemy that we can walk in balance and follow the Red Road. I even began to see the false front that was the macho tough guy. I always thought I had to stand on my own, without help not only from Tunkashila but also from other people. I never let people get too close to me, never let them see that I might have any weaknesses. Almost without realizing it, I began to let people in.

I knew I had a lot of catching up to do, a lot of holes to fill, after half a lifetime of wallowing around in my self-pity and trying to be the baddest guy around. All that time I had had the teachings within me—things from when I was growing up, my grandfather's and my people's teachings—but I was very stubborn. Ever since I was a young kid my Grandpa and others had told me of gifts that I would be given and good things I could do for the People. When I sobered up and turned my life over to Tunkashila, many things began to come to me. For many years I wondered why I didn't see the spirits and things that others saw in the Purification Lodge and in visions. My elders told me not to worry, that these things would come if they were supposed to. I discovered that when I truly turned things over to the Creator, the spirits began to make themselves known. If we are holding on to too many of our own things, too involved with ourselves, there is no room for the spirits to come into our lives. It is a process of purification.

As it turned out, Tunkashila gave me many things to do. I can only be grateful that he chose to help such a pitiful human being. In our ways there is no one that is beyond the Creator's help. I still don't feel worthy of some of the teachings I have been given, or the things with which I have been honored. Yet I know that it's not what we are or what we call ourselves that is important, but what we can bring that is of benefit to the People.

ᵭᵧ

In 1987 I returned to Fort Berthold to take part in the Sun Dance, which had been started up again among my people. By this time, I had two full years of sobriety behind me. The old man Ralph was there and his nephew Sammy. When the dance was ready to begin, Sammy came up to me and asked if I still had the bundle. I went and got the bundle, and then Sammy took me into a tipi.

There in the tipi were a few of my relations. My brother Kenny was there, and some of my Lakota relations. Sammy began to pray, and he told us that something that had been gone for eighty-six years was returning to the people. He told of how some people had seen a bear where I had been standing and watched an old-time warrior pass in front of the bear. He opened the bundle. A little rock that had been placed in there fell out, so he knew that I had not opened the bundle. Sammy took four little bags out of the bundle, and in them were four colors of paint. He began painting my face: blue around the jaw, black around the mouth, and then yellow and red above. That is all I can say about the bundle, except that in it are also two more paints that I have never worn; one of them is for war. Everyone was happy and some were crying, because something very ancient was returning to the People.

I was being painted as a Blackmouth, a society of brave men from the old days that had died out eighty-six years before; yet some of the songs and ways were still remembered. The old stories told that after the People came out of the earth, our legendary chief Good Furred Robe created the Blackmouth Society to protect the Corn People as they worked in the gardens. The Blackmouths were the protectors of the People; they were supposed to be the first and last in battle in defense of the village. The Mandan chief Four Bears was a leader of the society, and some have told me that the bear and the warrior the helpers saw when they came for me on the last morning of my fast were connected with him. The Blackmouth warriors were known far and wide for their bravery, and the plains tribes that came later modeled their warrior societies after them. At one point the Blackmouth warriors were approached by both the U.S. Army, who wanted to enlist them as scouts, and by Sitting Bull's Lakotas, our old-time enemies, to help drive the white men out of the territory. The Blackmouths refused them both.

Their society was also supposed to keep order in the village, to keep the peace and settle disputes and see that the people kept the village clean. They made sure that the ceremonies and sacred objects were respected. The Blackmouths made sure that everyone acted for the good of the tribe. If someone went out and scattered the herds before a tribal buffalo hunt, it could mean hunger for the People; the Blackmouths would find the one and they might break his arrows and his gun, whip him, or burn his tipi. They carried clubs and even had the power of life and death in extreme situations. But the Blackmouths were always under the direction of the elders.

The society accepted only mature men that had proven their bravery and showed consideration for all, including the aged, the young, the widowed, the orphaned, the helpless ones. When the government set up the Indian Police at my home, the Blackmouths lost their function and eventually died out. The Indian Police, however, was mostly made up of young men who had found a quick way to power and prestige and favor with the BIA agent, to whom they were answerable. They even turned on their own people, carrying out such orders as arresting our elders for performing ceremonies and forcibly taking children to be sent off to boarding schools. In the old days we governed ourselves through the councils and the societies, but our government, like so many other things, had been outlawed.

I was taken out before the People into the sacred Sun Dance circle, and Sammy told about what had returned to the people. I was also given a red eagle feather, which showed that I had been wounded in battle. Everyone was happy and lined up to shake my hand. During the dance a buffalo skull was hung from my back, and I was to stand through the whole dance, even while the other dancers rested. As I have said, we don't do these things to show our bravery, for we are pitiful, and I was once again given some of the power that flows from the Sacred Tree that helped my legs to stand and gave me moisture to fill my mouth.

There are two others that have dreamed of the Blackmouth now. I have a staff and a pipe that I carry as the symbol of the Blackmouth; the staff is carried in the procession that enters the Sun Dance circle. The staff has certain feathers, among them, the feathers of the raven. The blue in the Blackmouth face-paint honors the heron, for there is an old story that tells how one of the first Blackmouths was left to die after a battle, when his society brothers couldn't rescue him. His life was saved by a blue heron that came to him, used his beak to pull out an arrowhead, and then magically healed his wound.

The Blackmouth is an honor and something I take very seriously. It's not something I always feel worthy of. A Blackmouth is still charged with making sure that order and respect is observed at our sacred ceremonies, and that everyone is taken care of. They are the ones who carry the advice of the elders to the people. It would be a while before I overcame my prejudice against the white race, but over time I began to think of the Blackmouth as also representing the guardians of all people, helping to see that dignity and respect is shown to all peoples, and to all spiritual ways.

Within our spiritual ways, the sacred visions are not things that happened long ago; the Great Spirit now is the same Great Spirit that existed then, and that Spirit can still create wonders and touch the lives of the people. Many of my people's ceremonies and sacred bundles originated in the vision of one that had sacrificed and was favored by the spirits. These powers and visions are given so they may be used in service to the People, and from the People back to the Earth in a sacred circle.

# 11

# Building a Bridge

When I began to dance the Sun Dance in the 1970s, it was
with my people in mind. I danced for the return of our spiritual ways; I prayed for the Indian people who struggled for
their rights, for an end to all the alcohol and the hopelessness that were destroying us. I still dance for those things,
but at that time I was still filled with anger toward the white
man's world, the belly of the monster in which we live and
from which we cannot escape even if we tried. I see this
anger all the time in the Indians that drink. Think of what
we lost, and think how we're supposed to be happy with
the "civilization" that was imposed on us, a civilization
that has almost ruined this beautiful land. We had our own
spiritual ways; we had our own ways of government. We
didn't get these from a book, we got them from studying
nature, from natural laws. Before the invader came we had
no jails or mental institutions. Think of the holocaust that
took place in this land. We were supposed to forget; we were
supposed to disappear, yet we will never forget what happened on the Trail of Tears, the Long Walk, at Sand Creek,
and at Wounded Knee.

There are three things that the United States may never be forgiven for, and they still cause all kinds of problems, even though this country would like to forget them. One is the genocide of the Native peoples, the holocaust in which whole tribes dissappeared. Another is slavery. These two I always knew about, but a nephew of mine who is Japanese-American made me aware of another: the camps where his people were held during the Second World War.

I had a big chip on my shoulder, but at the same time I was afraid of white people; it goes back, I think, to my time in mission schools and my memories of cringing in fear in front of my teachers. I had trouble being around white people; I couldn't understand their attitudes, their ways of thinking. I had nothing good to say about white people.

In 1981 I finished a certification program in college for a degree in counseling, then found a job in Belleville, Illinois, working with Vietnam veterans. I specialized in delayed stress syndrome. I could relate to what they were going through; the things I experienced in Korea will be with me my whole life. But I was also starting to find that I was able to get inside the people I was counseling. I could see through their eyes and find ways to help, not through my own ideas and theories, but through their strengths and values. I didn't try to lay any of my learning on them; mostly I just listened. But these were white people and black people I was listening to, and I was hearing that they had problems just like mine. I began seeing them simply as people who felt all the pain and suffering and joy that we all share as human beings. But still I didn't know what to do with all the anger I had carried with me for all those years. I still couldn't be around white people outside of work and school. My life was out of balance.

I went back north and I talked to my father, and I talked to some of the elders at my home in Fort Berthold. I told them that I had to work every day with white people, and as a counselor I listened to all their problems, but how could I accept them, with the things they had done to our people and with their strange ways of thinking and acting? Each of the elders told me that I have to start living the true teachings of the Purification Lodge. In the darkness of the Purification Lodge, in the womb of the Mother, there is no race, only spirit, just as it was in the beginning. When we leave and when we enter the lodge we say "Mitakuye oyasin" in Lakota; among my Hidatsa people it is "Mada nugh baga aidsa"; and the Mandan say "Numak gagi aame." It means "All my relations." We are saying that we are related to all things; all beings are the children of one Creator, and we are but one of many children. None is above the other; no one is holier than another. The elders told me that until I could say those words and mean them in my heart, I could never walk in balance. If I used them and still had hatred in my heart, I could even hurt the ones I love. Those words are sacred, and I must take care of them.

The truth of this began to hit home with me as I continued my work in counseling. I saw more and more how we all share some of the pain and the sufferings and the struggles and the joys of this short time we are given. Still, my acceptance of the white race didn't happen overnight; like many things in my life, it was a long struggle.

—

Back in 1985, after I lost my job as an alcohol counselor at Fort Berthold, I was traveling around with the American Indian Movement. I was asked to go to Springfield, Missouri, where Leonard Peltier had been sent to a federal medical center because of health problems. Three carloads of us arrived in Springfield with our AIM flags flying; we were sent there to work with an attorney and organize support. There was supposed to have been a rally in front of the medical center the next day, but the next morning when we pulled up there was nobody around except one white woman all alone out there, walking back and forth and carrying a sign saying, "Free Leonard Peltier." At first I thought, "What is that crazy white woman doing out there all by herself?"

That woman became my wife, Daphne, and I owe much of my healing to her; so many things she has helped me to overcome. Daphne witnessed me at my worst, in my last year of drinking. She let me stay at the little place in the woods she had in the Ozark hills of southern Missouri. The next year we were married, and that place became a real home to me, and whenever I came home from work or from all my traveling I could walk around those woods and feel the peace and harmony of Creation. I also became close to Daphne's son, Chris Allen.

Archie Fire Lame Deer had come down before this and had built a sweat lodge on Daphne's land, to serve the spiritual people that might come to visit Leonard. I had already earned the right to pour water in the Purification Lodge, and of course I had known Archie for many years. Daphne and I always said that it was as if he knew someone would come along who could pour the water. My brother Kenny brought people down from St. Louis, and people from Kansas City would come to sweat, and white people would come along, too. Within the Purification Lodge I began to see these white people as real people. My own brother Kenny cried in the sweat lodge when he came down to visit us; he said he never thought he'd see the day when I would be in the sweat lodge with white people.

Sometimes it was harder to understand these white people that look to my people's ways. Once in 1985, Leonard had an appeal coming up in St. Louis, and we were going to hold a vigil through the whole trial. I was sent to a place in the National Forest where thousands of hippies were having a Rainbow Gathering down in the

Ozarks. I was supposed to recruit people to come to the vigil. The message that I was coming in my Thunderbird with North Dakota plates that said TRIBES got mixed up, and when we drove up they said, "Welcome Chief Thunderbird, chief of all the North Dakota tribes." No sooner had my buddy Cetan and I walked into that place than a buck-naked girl came and laid a big hug on me. "Welcome home, brother," she said. Cetan whispered to me, "I thought you said you didn't know these people!"

After I talked to some of the people there, I was feeling hungry. They told me that if I went to one of the free kitchens I could get a ham sandwich. Most of us Indians like our meat pretty well, so I went over there. They said, "Hold out your hand," and put some lettuce and stuff in my hand. "What's this?" I asked. "It's a 'hand sandwich,'" they told me. I never did get any meat that day.

It took me a while to get used to these long-haired gypsies, but "Chief Thunderbird" wound up leading a whole caravan of them up to St. Louis to help in the vigil. We created quite a stir when we'd stop in the little towns along the way. At first we were camped under the Gateway Arch, the monument to "westward expansion," which to us meant genocide, but the cops ran us out of there and made us camp in the park. We held sweat lodges, and elders such as Billy Good Voice Elk came to camp with us and share their teachings. Leonard Crow Dog, Archie Fire Lame Deer, Steve Roubideau, and others came, and for fifty-one days, while the judges ruled in Leonard's case, a sacred staff was carried day and night as we circled around the courthouse. In spite of new and old evidence of all kinds of government misconduct, Leonard's appeal was denied.

A couple of years after this I traveled to the Sun Dance that had started at Fort Berthold. I had just come from Crow Dog's Paradise, where only Native peoples had ever danced. When I got to my home I was shocked to see that a few white people there had danced with the people from my home—and one of them was my wife! I had been with white people in the Purification Lodge, I could now count a few white people among my friends, and I was married to a white woman, yet I had never imagined white people inside the Sun Dance circle. It was a shock at first, but that was the vision that began the dance there at my home. That dance is put on by those who follow the Wanagi Way. *Wanagi* means the spirit that lives in each of us, and the spirit that lives on after our death. In the spirit, they say, there is no color. I had to remind myself again of the words we say in the Purification Lodge, *mitakuye oyasin*—all my relations. A second dance began there, and on the fourth year a dream was fulfilled that all the four races would come into the Sacred Circle, and that year the black, the white, the red, and the yellow all danced beneath the Sacred Tree.

It wasn't long before more and more non-Indians and people with some Indian blood searching for their roots began to show up at our home in the woods in Missouri to take part in the sweats we had there. Those who came only as curiosity seekers soon satisfied their curiosity and left; as soon as they could say they had experienced a Native American ceremony, they never returned. Others stayed on, though, and they were eager to learn. Many that came were in the "helping" professions, and others came from alcohol and drug treatment centers. With both groups I began to see some lives that were truly turned around through the Purification Lodge.

The people in Missouri came to be my *tiyoshpaye*, my extended family. For anything I may have taught them, they have given back many times over in friendship. They know I'm a human being; they've seen both sides of me. They let me know when I'm not walking my talk. That was a big step for a "tough guy" that could never show anybody that he might have any weaknesses.

At our home in Missouri I pour the water in the Purification Lodge, but I've never claimed to be a teacher; I have never taken anyone on as my student. A teacher is someone who says, "This is the way it is." All I can do is share the things I was taught. Some of the people that came began to look on me as some kind of a chief or something, and I didn't want that. I told them to go to the different Sun Dances and Purification Lodges and learn respectfully from the elders and the ones who know the traditional ways. They began to learn the songs. We have shared together what it means to be a strong family. A few have even sun danced. They have learned that the Sun Dance Way is not an easy road.

After my wife, the next to dance was John, a white man who was involved in my people's political struggles. He had fasted for the vision to dance and came to my home up north. I knew just before this that I was to give away the pipe I had been given by Grandpa Henry Crow Dog. It would have been hard to believe just a few years before, but the pipe was to go to John. For a white man to carry the pipe was against everything I had believed in, yet that is what I was shown to do. John still didn't know if, as a white man, he should be sun dancing. I told him to go out on the butte there and to take tobacco in his hand and reach it to the heavens, but not to empty it in any direction, but to hold on to it and pray for guidance to the Four Directions and to the Mother and the Great Spirit and then release it to the winds. John danced that year just as I had begun, with no eagle feathers or anything, and for the first time I didn't see a man's color, but just a man dancing for the People. Before he left, the People had a giveaway, and John was given a blanket and some money for his journey home, for John has always given of what he has to my people, and he was given an eagle feather that was recorded at my home.

Before long, my people came to know my Missouri family, who would travel to the Sun Dances and sweat lodges.

I tried to teach them to know the culture first, so that they could get along with and bring something good to my people, instead of just taking away. At the same time, I could see the changes in the lives of these white people as they began to learn of my people's spiritual ways. They made a lot of mistakes while they learned, but they also made a lot of friends among my people. In some small way, I felt that there was beginning to be a bridge. My Indian people will never forget the things that were and are being done to us; but just as in my life, we can't live on resentments. The cultures will never come together completely, and that is how it should be, but we have to begin to build the bridges. Now it has come to where we are talking about the very survival of the Mother Earth, and we're going to make it or break it together.

When I first came to Missouri I worked at the Indian Center in St. Louis, and then at the one in Springfield. Then I worked at a boy's ranch for at-risk teenagers. Eventually I found a job as an alcohol and drug abuse counselor. Once again I was working with and counseling white people. I went back to school and became certified internationally. Daphne worked long hours as a children's librarian in Springfield, and sometimes I would work fifty or sixty hours a week, and then be gone from Friday to Sunday traveling. We worked hard together for the life we had there.

Many times I have wished that I could return to Fort Berthold to work with my own people, but too many people working in tribal government only remember me as a crazy drunk, or a militant, or both. I knew that between that and the usual tribal politics I wouldn't last long at any job there. I know that I have been criticized for not returning to work with my people. There are rumors that I run around the country, giving away ceremonies and charging money for spiritual teachings; I could never do this. Yet I know that there was a reason why I wound up living and working in the white man's world while still staying in close touch with my own people. I began to see that I was a bridge between cultures, among the many things Tunkashila had given me to do. I took what I had learned and shared with the wardens and staff of the prisons, where I have tried to bring the Purification Lodge and the pipe to those who have little hope. I have tried to bring some hope to the prisoners by letting them know that through these ways they can find freedom within themselves. Many times I have been humbled as I poured the water for the prisoners and listened as they prayed for their families, the nations, and the world outside their walls.

My brother Kenny fought for the religious rights of Native American prisoners long before it became a popular cause. In 1976, from inside of prison walls in Ohio, he fought for the right to wear his hair long and to carry a medicine pouch. He was beaten and kept in solitary confinement for ninety days for refusing to have his hair cut. Just before they were going to cut his hair forcibly, the court issued a restraining order. It was a precedent that paved the way for the rights of other Native prisoners.

Today, many states are backsliding on this issue, and Kenny works night and day for the laws that will give Native prisoners access to their ceremonies and instruments of worship. He still works hard for the American Indian Movement and for many other programs for his people.

My brother also worked for many years to see that the bones of our ancestors, which have been dug up and plundered, are returned to our people for proper reburial. I became involved in this important issue when I was asked to serve on the Missouri State Unmarked Human Burial

Commission. We now have a place in the state where our ancestors can be buried with the proper ceremonies. It's not always easy to get it across to the archaeologists and politicians that we feel as strongly about the remains of our ancestors as they would feel if their cemeteries were plundered and the bones scattered on the ground or left on a shelf in some museum or university.

Sometimes I feel I am a bridge from my own Indian people to our traditional ways through the Indian centers and organizations where there is so much in-fighting. I tell them that we are too few to be divided by petty disputes. I tell them that nothing will change until we go back to our own way of doing things. I tell them to open their meetings with prayer. I've fought for them to bring our spiritual teachings to the children. For some I have to explain that there is much more to being Indian than pow-wow dancing and costumes.

I have even seen this lack of unity among some of those in the Sun Dance and the Purification Lodge. Too often there are struggles for position and power, too many who are quick to judge others. One time at home I was discussing this with one of our elders, one of the last of the full-blood Mandans. He told me he didn't know all about this Sun Dance, but he felt that it was a good way and will grow stronger. But, he said, we need stronger people. In the old days the people put away their envy and bitterness and jealousy to be strong for the tribe, to be strong in our ceremonies so they might benefit the people and all things. He said we need "mean" people. He didn't mean angry people, of course; he meant people like our old-time warriors, those who were serious about their commitments.

With all the white people who were hungry for something, I saw it was placed in my hands that I could travel and make money and a name as a spiritual guru, running sweat lodges and giving away Indian names and things. There are ones who will do this. But I would always be afraid of bringing harm to myself, and most of all I would fear bringing dishonor to my people. If an elder comes and speaks or gives teachings, the people should pay his way and give all they can, but how could we ever set a price or charge for our spirituality, our sacred ceremonies? I'm happy with the simple life I have here.

Sometimes I wonder about those who come looking for spiritual answers in our Native ways. I wonder if they are ashamed of their own mothers and fathers, of their own people and their own ways. Sometimes I wonder about some of those with Cherokee blood and blood of other tribes; why are they seeking a northern plains way? Why don't they learn the language and ways of their own ancestors? Of course, with many tribes much has been lost, and many were forced to assimilate. Some people of those tribes who have found a spiritual walk through the Sacred Pipe and the Purification Lodge and the Sun Dance have gone on to relearn the ways of their own people.

I wonder what brings them to seek these ways, but then I remember the true teachings. If you are alone, if you have nowhere to turn, if you are disillusioned with all these other ways, if you know that you want to live in service to the People, if you have no spiritual walk and yet you know you are but a worshiper under the great Sun, privileged to walk on this Earth among the trees and the mountains and the rivers with gratitude to the Creator, then I will put my arms around you and say, "Welcome home. Come into the sacred Lodge of Purification. You belong here." This I will do, and this I hope others will do.

There are still Sun Dances where white people cannot dance, but at many they can come under the arbor and dance and offer their prayers and be a part of the Sun Dance circle in that way. This is according to the vision under which each dance is held. At some Sun Dances there are only Lakotas, for instance, and only Lakota is spoken; this is one way the old ways are kept alive. We are still trying to grow strong again ourselves in these ways. There are also those that still hold to the vision of the Ghost Dance, looking to the day when the Indian people and the Earth itself will be renewed. In other Sun Dances, white people may dance in the Sacred Circle if they come in the right way and come knowing why they are sun dancing.

Though I found myself becoming a bridge between two worlds, I have had a hard time when I see how some in the white culture come to my people. I've felt from some an attitude that we have been conquered and because they have read this or that book they have a right to our ways and instruments of worship and to use them any way they like.

Some come and try to change us: "Don't eat meat." "Use this crystal." There are a lot of funny stories I could tell about some of my *tiyoshpaye* as they learned the hard way about our culture. There are little things to know about us. For instance, if an elder is present you don't just stand there and look around, you go up and shake his hand. Don't stand over him or get down on your knees; sit beside him and know how to listen.

Many who come to our ceremonies have a romantic idea that all Indians are born into knowledge handed down through the generations. The truth is that many out there sun dancing and praying through the pipe come from broken families, alcoholic families, from prisons; they are just beginning to learn to walk the Red Road. For them these ways are not some kind of spiritual monkey business. Many owe their lives to these ways. Their lives have been turned around; through these ways I believe anyone can change. You may walk away from these ways of worship, but they will never leave you. Those who come should also know about the sacrifices that our ancestors made to keep our ways alive, and the battles that are still being fought for our religious freedom. They should know that we still fight for our rights as nations. We don't want hand-outs; we want self-determination, and to be self-sufficient.

I say, come to know the culture first. Without learning the culture, the pipe and sweat lodge are just things that people add to all the other things they don't know much about. They think that if they collect enough things they will somehow find wisdom. Come to know my people as people. Don't come only looking to take. Don't come just at the start of a ceremony and leave when it's over. Share in the work; share in the fellowship. Be able to listen. Leave your books and your ideas at home; don't try to fragment our ways and mix the pieces with all kinds of other ways, as was done with Christianity. If you are beginning to learn our ways, don't seek an instant rebirth as a person that now knows everything. There are steps we take, and in our ways the rights to perform certain ceremonies are given only af-ter the steps have been taken, after there is a true under-standing. Then we become gifted with the things we need to help our lives. Take it easy, you have a long way to go. But the Red Road is not an easy road. It is living your life in service to the People, to the Creator, and to the Mother Earth. I always tell people that I'm not doing them any favors by showing them the Red Road.

I see many changes coming. More and more white people will come seeking a spiritual connection to this Earth, and I truly believe that the teachings of the Red Road and the Sacred Pipe and the Lodge of Purification, the ways taught by the White Buffalo Calf Woman and the visionaries of many tribes, will come to be the salva-tion of this Earth; for the basic teachings are not an Indian way, but the way of human beings, of being people on this Earth. We are going to make it or break it together. They say that long ago all were within the Sacred Circle, around the council fire: the white, the black, the yellow, and the red together, with love for the Mother, but that different ones wandered away from the circle, even many of the red race. Great things were done by those that wandered away, but they could have done those great things and not have left the Mother. Yet a few kept the sacred fire going, the council fire, the fire of life, so that it would not die out forever.

There is a reason why the Sacred Pipe was kept through all the massacres and all the attempts to crush our spiritual ways, and why it is now growing stronger every day. There are prophecies that speak of the seventh generation from the coming of the white man as being the one that will see the big changes that are coming. This is the seventh generation coming up, and these are the people we must teach so they will do things right this time, so that they will keep in mind what they will leave for the next seven generations that will follow them. This is how we are taught to live on this earth: we should look to how our decisions and actions will affect the seventh generation to come.

In this year a white buffalo calf was born, and I believe that it marks the beginning of the purification, when the Earth will be renewed. It will be a natural process of the Mother Earth's healing. The Earth will survive; the Earth will survive for eons of time as she heals, even if we are not here. She has already survived for ages and ages without us. But through the pipe we may come to know how to survive this purification. I don't know in what form we will survive, but one day, I believe, this Earth will be a paradise again. One day we will come together in the Sacred Circle, the circle we are all born into as the children of one Father and one Mother.

〰

Sometimes words like the following just come to me, and I write them down. I don't know what I'm writing until I read it afterward, but I feel that they come from Tunkashila. This is one of those things that was given to me, like a little vision:

*I feel part of the bridge is the Sun Dance.*
*A woman through me is the power*
*and will be the power for hers to come true.*
*The non-Indian that dances either in the Sacred*
*Hoop or under the arbor*
*who feels the drum and song and smokes the pipe*
*will be one with the Earth,*
*especially if she has entered into the ritual of the*
*buffalo.*
*They have gone into our skins and our hearts*
*and made one with love to the power*
*and the world of giving and knowledge inside*
*ourselves*
*so we may live, touch, taste, smell, see, hear,*
*and walk in balance,*
*to have this power to be of service to others.*

*A person must enter*
*and to enter must leave.*
*To come you must go.*
*To heart dance you must believe.*
*You will remember what was yours at the*
*beginning.*
*Believe and you will find peace and happiness.*
*Remember, do not confuse your earth body*
*with the past teachings of man.*
*Yours is the teachings of the Earth, the Sky,*
*and everything in between.*
*This is your true Mother, your true Father.*
*Give over to the strength and happiness of inner self.*
*To them these things of natural life are yours;*
*then from you to the People,*

*from the People back to the Earth,*
*and from this strength to all in between.*
*This voice you know.*
*This instruction you know.*
*Walk in balance,*
*and be of your own taking and giving.*

*You are braided to help me tie Grandfather's*
*children together.*

TWO RAVENS

# Epilogue:

# SHAKING HANDS WITH THE GREAT CHIEFS

## by Robert Liebert

Louis Two Ravens Irwin died on January 22, 1995. His last years kept him as busy as any three people should be. It was as if he were trying to make up for lost time, taking advantage of ten years of full sobriety during which he tirelessly worked as an alcohol and drug counselor, continued his education, traveled to the prisons to bring the pipe and sweat lodge to those who had lost their freedom, and never missed a year of the Sun Dance. His dedication to the American Indian Movement continued. He counseled and aided his friends and relations and Native American people across the country. In Missouri, where he was like a fish out of his cultural waters, Louie became a respected community leader who spoke out for the diversity of all people in an area that had a long history of racism.

Despite his honors and accomplishments, Louie never let you think he was more than a human being. For better or worse, Louie was always up front. Whether he was wearing a business suit or his Sun Dance regalia, he was the same person. Those who knew him in his last years remember how he could set a whole roomful of people at ease and laughing with his easy smile and his stories. He could also give the briefest, most devastating look if something wasn't done in a respectful way. It made you want to crawl in a hole. He could be great to be around, and he could be the biggest grouch in the world.

Louie was not a saint, and he still did some bad along with a lot of good. His wife, Daphne, may have come close to being a saint, being with a man who could at times be very hard to live with. It wasn't easy, either, being married to a spiritual leader and opening her home, day or night, to relations, Native leaders, and people seeking advice, help, or spiritual answers. Daphne knew that Louie was a man who belonged to the People, yet she always maintained that she received as much as or more than she gave in their life together.

At his home in Missouri Louie had found peace. After a stint of traveling to the places he was called, there was nothing he loved better than to walk and work in the woods that surrounded his and Daphne's cabin. Louie always cut wood, hauled rocks, and worked right alongside those who would show up to take part in their sweat lodges, and he always stressed the sharing of the work and the concept of family and unity. By example he taught that we don't come to the Lodge of Purification just to take something away, but that the teaching of *mitakuye oyasin,* that we are all related, had to be lived.

The white people and Native Americans who came to Louie and Daphne's knew that Louie wasn't going into the sweat lodge for their benefit; he was just sharing what he would be doing even if no one was there. Louie started to teach some of the sweat lodge songs and the things that should always be respected. He shared the things he thought he had the authority to speak on, and otherwise he told the people to go to the places where they could learn from the elders. He made people more aware of their cultural biases and attitudes, so that those who went to his people could go ready to learn from another culture. He opened the way for some of the white people there to go to the Sun Dance. Yet Louie didn't necessarily take to every white person as his long lost brother or sister. He didn't go around giving away names and pipes to people who asked for such things. In his last few years he became increasingly less inclined to share his people's ways with those who he felt weren't prepared or weren't serious about receiving them. But it was a sign of how far he had come that he spoke openly, often in the face of much criticism, for the careful sharing of the Sun Dance and Lodge of Purification teachings with all races.

Louie laid his convictions on the line with his own people one year at Crow Dog's Sun Dance. A man from France who had carefully followed the ways for many years and had learned the Lakota language was joining the Sun Dance. Many there at Crow Dog's Paradise were uneasy. There had been African Americans with Indian blood, and Asians, and even Buddhist monks that had danced there, but never a white man. The Frenchman was making the sacrifice of being pierced to the buffalo skulls and dragging them around the Sun Dance circle. Most of the sun dancers that pull the skulls are supported by friends and loved ones who walk alongside or follow behind them. The Frenchman was all alone as he dug his feet in the earth and struggled to make his way around the circle.

Louie would later say that he didn't have it in his mind to make a statement, but that as he witnessed the struggle of the Frenchman he once again saw no skin color, only a man who had come into the Sun Dance with no eagle feathers, at the back of the line with the children, a man who had come to dance for the People. Louie went out and walked beside the Frenchman, and then others got up to walk in support behind him.

⇌

In 1992 Louie told those around him that he had had the same dream four times and knew he must carry it out. He saw himself on a fast at his home in North Dakota, and he saw just where and how he was to carry it out. It was to take place on top of Thunder Butte, a very high, steep-sided hill and landmark on the reservation about which many old stories had been told, as it was said to be the home of the Thunderbirds.

Many tribes speak of the Thunder Beings that travel with or bring the rain clouds, thunder, and lightning. In the stories of the Mandan they are spoken of as giant birds that fly in the storm clouds and shoot lightning from their eyes. Thunder Butte is a place Louie's people go to with much respect and even fear. The spirits told him that he would take no food offerings up there and that he was to be pierced and tied to the buffalo skulls. A large area on top of the butte was to be marked in the Four Directions as his place for fasting, and he was to walk the circle with the buffalo skulls until he was released. This was an ancient way of fasting among his Mandan and Hidatsa people.

Louie was pierced to the skulls on top of Thunder Butte and was soon released. He decided to stay until the next morning. His real test was yet to come, for that night the Thunder Beings came, and those who watched the butte say the lightning that night was incredibly intense on all sides around Thunder Butte, yet no lightning struck the top of the butte, where Louie fasted. Louie never spoke of what he saw that night, except that the lightning scared him to death and that there were spirits dancing all around him. The spirits of the buffalo also came, and he could hear them and smell them and feel them all around. When the elders came after Louie the next morning, they were amazed to see that around his place of fasting the grass was beaten down in a large circle as if a herd had trampled it down in the night, and for a long time after, the ground remained as if many people or animals had trampled the grass in a large circle. Though Louie didn't reveal all that he had seen and felt that night, he told those that were close to him that he had been released from some things; maybe some things for which he felt shame or remorse, but things that he had carried around for a long, long time.

⟜

Soon after, the Thunder Beings visited again at a Sun Dance held on a high butte above the lake that was once the Grandmother River. The only thing between earth and sky was the Sacred Tree, and Louie was pierced and tied to the tree all through the night. Those that looked up at the butte that night saw the massive storm cloud that sat above the butte, sending bolt after bolt of lightning to earth. All night the wind blew with a great fury, and those of us in the sun dancer's tipi each had to hold on to a pole for dear life, just to keep us and the tipi from blowing off the butte and into the lake far below. In his frustration one of the dancers shook his fist at the storm. We could hear the crack and smell the electricity as the lightning hit his fist and traveled up the young man's arm. He was lucky to be alive, and the next day he had to be doctored in the Purification Lodge.

All through that terrible night Louie sat, connected to the tree. But once again, the lightning never struck Louie, even though the Sun Dance tree was the highest object for miles around. Louie never spoke of what went on that night either, except that at times he felt like he was back on the cold, dark hill in Korea.

⟜

Only a few short months later, Louie lay in the hospital, where he was diagnosed with cancer, with only a few months to live. At first Louie went through all the terrible fears and doubts that anyone would experience. One day he sat up and told those around him that he now knew that either way he would win; either in beating his disease or by going the spirit way and having the honor of shaking hands with the great chiefs. That is how he lived out his days: telling those around him to be thankful to the Creator for every breath, every heartbeat.

One day as Louie lay in the hospital, three people from off the streets of Springfield stepped quietly into his room. They said they had heard about Louie's illness and risked the walk across town; usually the cops would haul them back to the skid row part of town, where the street people were kept in line.

They had met Louie when they had been sent into treatment, and they said that he was the only counselor who had made a difference in their lives. Though they hadn't conquered their alcoholism, he had taught them to live with some dignity; they said he had taught them to help others and never to steal. For this they would always be thankful to him. Then they slipped out as quietly as they had come. We were only beginning to learn how many lives Louie had touched. Many more would come forth after his passing.

Louie was given three months to live, but the doctors didn't know that they had a warrior on their hands. Louie sun danced the next year at Crow Dog's Paradise, then later at Fort Berthold, wearing a headdress that had been made of a coyote skin and stepping high, the way he had always danced. He looked like a fierce old-time warrior.

Throughout his life Louie knew he was given powers and protection through the Thunder Beings but was wary of their great power. A Navajo medicine man told him that his sickness was caused by absorbing too much of the Thunder Beings' power. Some may have thought he was suffering for things he had done. Others spoke of how many healers can be overcome by taking on too much of the pain and sickness of others. There are many theories but no answers to why a life seems to be cut short. That is in the hands of the Great Mystery.

Louie struggled on for a year and a half after his diagnosis. He took advantage of both Native and Western herbs and means of healing. Sometimes he looked tired and weak, but when he wasn't recovering from the awful effects of the chemotherapy he had chosen to take, he would be on his feet and look strong and would go out, traveling hundreds of miles to men's and women's prisons, continuing his fight to bring the instruments and ways of worship to the Native American prisoners, to those with no hope. He continued his counseling, he ran sweat lodges, he continued to fight for Leonard Peltier's release, to fight for unity in the American Indian Movement. He cared for his large extended family. He reburied the bones of ancestors that had been dug up. Sometimes he gave talks, and if he sensed a high level of ignorance among the white people he was speaking to he could easily switch back to the radical AIM warrior and wake them up to what had been done and what is done every day to the Native American peoples.

There was also the daily spiritual walk of seeking balance, of trying to walk his talk. He had proven himself in many ways as a warrior, and now he sought peace within himself and with the world. Ever since he had come to Missouri he had been seeking another kind of balance. Archie Fire Lame Deer had told him that there was indeed a balance he needed as one who had always seen himself as the macho tough guy, that he needed to seek the feminine nature and be close to the Mother Earth. When he was home in Missouri he would spend quiet times out among the trees, "those who stand praying." In his last years it wasn't un-

usual to go by and see the tough old warrior carefully carrying out of the house little bugs and spiders. Not long before
he died, Louie gave away all his guns.

~

Louie entered the Lodge of Purification for the last time.
It had taken every bit of his strength to make it out there,
and he was helped to a place by the door. For days Louie
had been in another place, closer to the next world than
the one we know. But Louie looked up and gazed around
the circle of people and then flashed that mischievous
smile of his. Louie had come back for that moment, and
we didn't know he was saying good-bye.

"Always be grateful," he said. Louie wanted to sing
the song he had been given at Sun Dance that year, a
thanksgiving song to be sung both in times of joy and in
times of sorrow and pain, thanking the Creator for the
blessings and honor of being alive and for the lessons we
are given. In a voice that was weak but sincere, he began:

*Wakan Tanka, Tunkashila*
*pilamaye, pilamaye . . .*

Great Spirit, Grandfather,
Thank you, thank you . . .

~

Back at his home in the north, the spirits came into the
Purification Lodge and told the people there that Louie's
time was approaching. Three of them traveled down to
the Ozarks: Uncle Tony and his wife, Rosella, and Rosella's
sister, Grandma Sadie, who led the last Sun Dance, where
Louie danced with the coyote skin. Tony is a leader of the

Low Cap clan, which is associated with the Thunder Beings, and is the man who is charged with splitting the clouds at Sun Dance so there will be fair weather.

The last few days had been hard on Louie, as he drifted closer to the next world. At times he was in Korea and other places and with people who had gone before. Sometimes he even spoke in the voice of a young boy. It was almost as if he had to walk the whole circle of his life and live his battles once more in order to make a final peace.

In spite of all the encouragement those around him gave to seek one or another healer, Louie knew his time was up. One of his nieces in his *tiyoshpaye,* Kerry, had died just a few days earlier after a long battle with cancer. Louie had told her on the phone to wait for him, to be happy, and that he would see her soon.

The day before Louie passed on, it had snowed more than a foot, and in the midst of the falling snow there was lightning and thunder—a truly *heyoka* day. That night was almost as clear and cold as a North Dakota winter night. While we held vigil we would wander out now and then to look up at the frosty stars, and in the darkness Grandma Sadie told some of the old stories of the spirits and people that had journeyed to the heavens to become the stars. In the dark woods Tony had seen the shadowy form of a young boy moving among the trees.

Louie had finally found peace and rested quietly. In the darkness just before dawn our vigil was ended. Louie looked around once, gave Daphne's hand a squeeze, and breathed a last breath. There was a great silence; it was more like witnessing the miracle of a birth than a death. Tony told us how the old ones say that many of the traditional people pass on at that hour, to greet the great Sun. It was the hour when the crier calls for the sun dancers to arise and enter the Lodge of Purification, ready to greet a new day within the Sacred Circle of the Sun Dance.

⟿

Not long before Louie's passing, he was visited by his son John. They had seen each other only a few times since their days on the streets of Los Angeles. Their previous visit, years before, hadn't gone well. They were both still drinking, and John still had a lot of resentments. During this last visit, though, they shared many good words. They discovered how much their lives had paralleled. John, too, had endured a rough military stint in a Special Forces unit. There were the battles with alcohol and racism. Both had returned to the ceremonial ways of their people. John is one who carries a whip at the dances of his people at San Juan Pueblo. Men who have beaten their wives, drunk and caused trouble, or otherwise disrupted the life of the Pueblo risk being ceremonially whipped before the people. The whip, like the Blackmouth staff John's father carried, was something that had to be carried with nonattachment and with the hearts of the People in mind.

Very early on the morning that Louie passed on, John awoke and saw Louie standing by his bed. His father and he walked to a beautiful waterfall. When John looked into the waterfall it became a mirror. In it he could see a huge tree with spreading branches. In the branches he could see many faces. Louie told him, "These are your ancestors and your people." John looked at the tree again, and he could see that the faces of the oldest ancestors were at the top of the tree. Down further were those that had passed on not long before, and at the bottom were the faces of those yet to be born. All were moving up: moving up the Sacred Tree, reaching toward the Great Spirit.

⟿

For those of us that had witnessed Louie's passing, the loss of our relation didn't hit home until we had cooked breakfast early that next morning. Daphne had prepared a plate for the spirits, as Louie had always directed to be done before the family ate. Alongside the spirit plate that Daphne had left on the altar before the sweat lodge she had placed a cup of coffee and a cigarette for Louie. When she returned we truly missed the one who had loved to laugh and joke and tell stories and sing the good songs with the people around him.

For a short time Tony broke down and cried, telling us that it was OK to cry, to honor our memories of our uncle, but not to call on him too much, not to cry too much, for the spirit would be restless and had to begin its journey home. There were many places, he said, that he had to visit before his spirit could begin its journey. Tony even directed us to place some of Louie's clothes on the sweat lodge fire, beginning the process of letting go.

Under a blue sky we smoked the Sacred Pipe, and then Tony brought out an old sacred medicine of his Mandan people: a whistle shaped like a turtle from the seas. Tony blew on the whistle four times. Four times the turtle called, and suddenly from somewhere above came the answering cry of an eagle.

⚬⚬

There are old Mandan stories that tell of how long ago the People lived near the Gulf Coast and met a people with fair skin who traveled in boats. For a time they lived together, sharing food and songs and ceremonies. The fair-skinned people stayed in the south while the Mandans began their journey up the Grandmother River. One prophecy said that one day the fair-skinned people would come from the south to be with them once more.

It may not have been the fulfillment of ancient prophecies, but the adopted family of Two Ravens did head north in a caravan. His brother Kenny drove with the casket, honoring Louie's wish that he be placed in a plain wooden box and be driven home to Fort Berthold in the back of a pickup by his friends. Together with the relations from the north, they laid to rest the man who had built many bridges among the People, in a quiet cemetery where the winds blow over the prairie, overlooking the People's ancient home near the waters of a lake where lies the spirit of the Grandmother River, waiting.

The next year at Crow Dog's Sun Dance a chair with Louie's picture was placed in the Sun Dance circle, along with a blanket, his moccasins, and some of his sacred things. Before the dance began, the ceremony was held in which all those who had lost someone in the year since the last dance stand while the people pass before them and symbolically and literally wipe their tears away. This is done so the mourners may leave some of their grief behind before the beginning of the Sun Dance, the beginning of a new cycle for those who follow the Sun Dance Way.

During a break in the dance, Louie was honored as his adopted mother, Ednah New Rider Weber, read a tribute to him. The dancers, who had been resting under the arbor, suddenly got up and went into the circle and sang the AIM song with fists raised. The song is one that has been adopted by many tribes, a song to give courage to those who fight for their people. Now they sang for the warrior and Sun Dance chief who had passed on. Louie never called himself a Sun Dance chief, but he had danced at Crow Dog's Paradise for twenty years, and that is what the People called him. No longer could the dancers be inspired by his high-stepping, tireless energy while, as Louie said, he "danced for the glory of God." He danced proud but humble. He made people feel at ease. He gave the people courage. Louie had joined the others who had danced there and passed on, and so he became a part of the generations, the ancestors whose lives nourish the Sacred Tree, a part of the circle that never ends.

### To My Family, and to All People of Creation

*It was known forever,*
*for all time known and imagined before*
*and since the first day of Creation,*
*that we were and are the children of this Holy*
*Creation.*
*That we are here, have been here, and will always*
*be here;*
*we the children of all colors*
*from all directions from the center.*
*This center is our own body, our own being,*
*and from the beginning we were born holy*
*and leave this holiness only of our own choosing;*
*therefore the thought of loneliness comes only*
*when we have left this holiness.*

*We are all preparing,*
*all of us;*
*we prepare for the eventual change of worlds:*
*our "death" here on this side,*
*a death that is in fact a true rebirth*
*and a time of thankfulness,*
*for we shall live, visit, love, and be with*
*those we have longed to meet and have long missed,*
*those that went to the other side before us.*

*So have no fear, no regret,*
*for we have all had our chance on this side,*
*and if we were true to the belief in the Great Spirit*
*then we will go to the Ghost Villages without*
*shame.*
*Our eyes will be clear*
*and when the Holy Grandfather greets us*
*our fear and loneliness will bring a smile*
*and a true gratefulness.*

*So keep in mind that until this day or night comes*
*live, love, laugh, and be real to your self;*
*live each day as if you were on top of the mountain*
*bringing all of the Great Spirit's creation,*
*all beings, all people,*
*into and unto your love.*
*Live completely with joy and thankfulness*
*right up to the time you enter the other side.*
*We will never leave each other*
*for if we have lived in a good way*
*we will all have fond memories.*

ALL MY RELATIONS YOU ARE
*Louis Two Ravens Irwin*
*November 10, 1993*

# Appendix A:

# WALKING THE SACRED CIRCLE

*Louis Two Ravens Irwin often said that for wisdom and knowledge we shouldn't look to humans as the final word. We must look to the Creation, to the Creator, and most things we must learn for ourselves, the hard way. He would never claim that the things he was taught or given were his teachings. They were the "ways of the ways," ancient teachings about finding balance and meaning in our lives, about how to respect ourselves and all living things. The following was gleaned from the talks he gave as a substance abuse counselor and in the prisons, and from a talk he gave to Native American students at Haskell College in Lawrence, Kansas. Louis was always the first to admit that he struggled every day to find the balance he spoke of. But everywhere Louis spoke, the people knew that here was someone who had lived the things he said.*

Despite what you may read, the Native American people have always been monotheistic. For my people there is

148

only one Great Spirit, so great that it covers the entire universe and yet so small that it is in each of us, in the smallest creature that walks or crawls. That is why we cannot respect the Creator without respecting the Creation. The dominant culture says that we are heathens, that we worship idols. It is true that we have our instruments of worship, like our Sacred Pipe, but we do not worship these things; rather, we pray through them to our Creator. Tunkashila knows that as human beings we need something that is real that we can hold on to, and so he has given us these ways and instruments of worship so that we may stay close to him. Each of the peoples of the earth was given their own ways, according to their own understanding.

The Creator made all the powers in the universe, and in them is a part of his power. There is a power in the Earth, and we call the Earth our Mother, because our bodies and everything we need to live she provides for us. From our Father we receive protection. And so we say that every living thing is related as the children of one Father and one Mother, the Father Sky and the Mother Earth. Each of us are but one of many children. All things must be respected as if they were truly our relations. None is above the other; none is holier than any other. As long as we are alive and walk between the Earth and Sky we have our spiritual parents and many, many relations, and remembering this has helped me many times when I felt truly alone.

As the children of one Father and one Mother, we are each of us born holy. This is very different from the view that we are born in sin. If there is a hell, it is the one we create for ourselves here on this Earth. We can no more conceive of a God that would punish us forever than we can think of a parent who would want to punish her child for all eternity.

When we are in our mother's womb, the first thing we hear is the heartbeat; it is the heartbeat of our Mother

Earth, the heartbeat we share with all living creatures. This connection, this unity with all things, we know from before our birth. This natural way of life we know. It is the drum within us, and when it beats to the drum outside us we know we have found that balance, that connection once more.

Since we are born holy, there is nothing we need to become, nothing we need to acquire to become a spiritual person. In the dominant culture there is always a big push to acquire something. Our path is more of a returning to the oneness and harmony we knew from before we were born. We are born into a sacred circle; this is our birthright. The path itself, our daily spiritual walk, is the only goal.

In my counseling I try to look past the crazy person, or the person that does crazy things, to the place inside each one of us that is good, the place where there is balance. There are gifts that the Creator gives to each and every one of us; we are born with the capacity to love, to perceive, to understand, and to be sensitive to joy and laughter and sadness and to the needs of others.

The Creator gave us human beings free will. You could say he turned us loose on the Earth to experience many things. Through the things we experience, the things that are done to us, and the things we have done to others, we begin to feel hurt, anger, fear, mistrust. For some, childhood can be a terrible experience. We begin to lose the balance, the connection we had. We can no longer see the Sacred Circle. There is a lot of talk now about the "inner child," and my people know of this, but we also say that the child has to grow up, too. As a counselor I can't make you change, I can only try to listen and see through your eyes and maybe help you find the power that is inside you, the power to change. This power is within you alone. I can't help you with the things that happened forty years ago, and you can't help them either; all we can change is right now. And so to begin our spiritual walk, in spite of all the things we were dealt, we must face the responsibility we have as the true children of our spiritual Mother and Father. We are given only one life; this isn't a dress rehearsal. What are we going to do with this life we are given?

We begin to do the will of the Creator when we make a conscious change for the good. It is up to us to take that first step to reclaim what is our birthright, our spiritual self. We must decide that we are going to begin our spiritual walk. Our walk begins from where we are right now, with all our problems and fears. Each moment, each day is a part of our spiritual walk.

As we begin our spiritual walk we find that there are many holes we start to stumble into. They may be things we have done to others, or that others have done to us, or they may be the things inside us that keep us from growing. The things in the past are just shadow memories, but like a shadow they still follow us around. They can cause a lot of pain. Before we can continue to walk we must begin to fill in the holes, because as we come around the circle of our lives we will stumble in that hole again, and maybe it will be bigger next time. It is like fear: You can run from it, but you can never outdistance it because it is inside us. All you can do is face it. This was my grandfather's teaching.

It is easy to get stuck. I once worked with a man whose wife had left him a couple of years before. He hadn't even heard from her since then, but just the mention of her name would send him into orbit. He'd go crazy just from hearing her name. He had given away his power to her, and she was off in California somewhere and didn't even know she had that power.

But day by day we can begin to fill in the holes. When we find ourselves out of balance we may have to seek and find the holes that we didn't even know were there. So first we throw out the garbage, decide to come with a clear mind; then we seek to forgive others. We try to make amends for the things we have done. It isn't always possible to do this directly with the ones we have hurt; sometimes we have to make amends by the way we treat the ones that are in our lives now. We must remember, though, that it is not our words but our actions that will begin to fill in the holes. It is changing that begins to fill in the holes. We've got to be real within ourselves, so we can be real to others.

Many people will never take that first step to become what we were meant to be; we will turn to our closetful of excuses or our pills or our bottle before we ever take that step. Or better yet, we want someone else to do it for us. Instead of dealing with our problems we'll join a new religion or find a new relationship. Even if our life is totally out of balance we still think we are the ones in control of our lives. But who's really in charge here? Even if we don't know what "God" is, we surely must know that we are not the Creator or the controller of this life. We don't control the things that happen in our life. Usually it takes hitting bottom or some kind of crisis to realize that we've lost control, that we've never been in control, and yet we'll still try to hang on to that control to the bitter end. Even after we have begun our spiritual walk we can give up our faith and go along just fine for a while: "I can fake it till I make it." I was one of those hard cases.

Yet we can have faith in the Creator, in God, and still run our lives entirely on self-will. We'll find that we won't get very far on our spiritual walk until we finally decide to turn our lives over to the Creator. We do the things we need to do to begin; we make amends where we can, we learn to forgive, and the rest we have to turn over to Tunkashila. When we smoke the Sacred Pipe in ceremony we put our prayers in there and then we send them to the Creator; we turn them over to the higher power.

Prayer is our conscious contact with the Creator. Tunkashila already knows our hearts and minds, and so we must be honest, and so we must be humble. Phoniness, fear, dishonesty, and rationalization all get in the way of this contact. We will try to make bargains with Tunkashila: if I go to church, if I do a good deed, if I sun dance . . . We think we can just keep those little secrets and negative emotions and jealousies, the things we think no one knows about. We think that these are what we really are. This kind of "stinking thinking" was all I had for a long time, until one day I found I had a God-given conscience and felt truly bad about something that no one even knew about. But even our character defects are really just instincts gone astray. There is a balance of the good and the bad in us and in the world; when we turn our lives over they will begin to fall into place, into a balance. You will go where you need to go. To win we must surrender, to live we must die, to come we must go.

And so we begin to pray. We don't always pray for things; sometimes we can only pray for the strength to cope. Elders have told me that it is good to pray at least twice a day: to pray in the morning for strength for the day ahead, and in the evening to give our prayer of thankfulness. My elders also told me that life isn't always fair, and that I would have hard times, but that I would find the strength to endure. The most important thing is to maintain that conscious contact with God.

Then we should listen deep within. This is an important part of praying, because deep within us we will feel and know the truth. Deep within us is a higher power that communicates with the Creator. We have a God-given conscience. In the meantime we can't sit back and wait for knowledge or an interpreter to come to us; we must seek it within ourselves, because the truth is already inside us. No one can walk the path of our life and learn for us.

Because we turn our lives over doesn't mean that we are nothing. We have many gifts and abilities, but we want to use them in the right way. We turn our lives over to Tunkashila and a funny thing happens: suddenly we find that we are so dependent on the Creator that we are independent, that we are truly free. We are free from the fears and jealousies and little secrets. This is how we begin to make our invisible shield of protection, with the help of Tunkashila; the shield is invisible yet real. Suddenly all those things can't control us, we don't get sucked in, and our enemies can no longer take our power. No one is strong enough to take away our faith. As human beings we will still feel these negative emotions and experience things we think are negative. But soon you will get to where you can go on with your life, with your spiritual walk, and soon nothing can come between us and our Creator.

In my counseling work I often draw out for people the Sacred Circle of our life. This circle is our spiritual walk; it is the Red Road. We each have our own walk. We each own our birth and our death, yet it is a circle, because death is only a rebirth, a change of worlds. Our children and the things we leave behind us continue the circle. Each of us is born at a different place on the circle. We each are born with certain strengths and certain gifts; other things we have to struggle for. It seems like we always expect others to see things the way we do, to see from where we are on the circle, to walk right in our same footsteps, yet no one can walk our path for us, and we must give others the freedom to walk their own paths.

The things I put in the circle are just some of the many ways to talk about it. Four is a sacred number to my People, and at the Four Directions could be placed the four stages of our life: birth, youth, old age, death, and back to birth. Or there could be the four seasons—many things. When I speak of finding balance in our lives I place at the Directions the four gifts that each of us are given by the Cre-

## *Our Spiritual Walk*

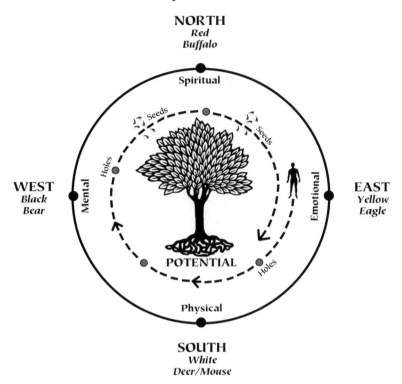

**NORTH**
*Red*
*Buffalo*

**WEST**
*Black*
*Bear*

**EAST**
*Yellow*
*Eagle*

**SOUTH**
*White*
*Deer/Mouse*

ator at birth, and they are also the four ways in which we grow. These four we must always try to keep in balance. They are the physical, the emotional, the mental, and the spiritual. If only one is out of balance, the whole person is out of balance.

If you don't take care of your body and you get very sick, all the others are out of balance. We may be drawn to be spiritual, but we may lack compassion for others, or our thinking may be all wrong. Then things are out of balance. We may have to travel the circle back to the emotional and work out our feelings. When I work with

Indian people I also place the four colors and the animals for each Direction. They can understand the strengths and teachings they represent. The animals show us ways to be in balance, for they live the ways that were given to them by the Creator.

At the center of the circle is where we find balance. It is the place within us where the Great Spirit dwells. In the center of the circle I put a Tree. In the Sun Dance it is the Tree of Life that sends out its seeds, its blessings of life to the Four Directions, to all living things. In the circle of our life it begins as a little seed. This is our potential, a seed that we are born with, and like a tree we are born to become what we are meant to be. But we are born into the circle stronger in some of these gifts than others; others we have to struggle to gain, but we will grow. Sometimes we are given real challenges in the physical, the emotional, the mental, and the spiritual, but like the winds of the Four Directions, they go to making the strength, the balance of the tree. I think many cultures have something like the saying "Anything that doesn't kill you only makes you stronger." My people also used to say that a turtle has to stick his neck out to go anywhere. In the Sun Dance we use a cottonwood tree that is forked at the top to stand for the positive and negative, the male and female, the bad and the good. Yet the two are really one, and both are needed for the balance of the tree.

As we grow in the four gifts and learn to balance them, we begin to nourish that sprout, that potential, and the tree begins to grow. Eventually it will bear fruit, and the tree will send out its seeds to the Four Directions so that we can continue to grow in the four ways. These are gifts that are given to us; sometimes they are lessons. If we receive a gift, we have to take care of that gift; we have to understand it before we give it away. One time one of my nieces was given a gift from Tunkashila in the Purification Lodge. I told her that she wasn't to tell anyone about her gift or use her gift for one year. After a while she came to me and said she realized she was having a lot of trouble with the dominant-culture point of view that if you have something great you're supposed to tell everybody about it right away and start using it. This is how the truth becomes diluted and weakened. After a while she began to understand that the gift has to be nourished and understood. The gift is a seed, and to give it away before it is understood is like lopping off a branch of the tree before it ever bears fruit. We can't give something we don't have.

Along the way we will find help. We have allies among the spirits, good spirits that can help and teach us. Each of us also has an inner guide that can help us and guide us through our lives. People will enter our lives who will be our teachers. Our enemies can be our greatest teachers. Our Creator also gave us instruments and ways of worship so we can remain close to him. There are those who will always seek a teacher, or will follow only one teacher, yet a teacher can only point the way to the knowledge we already have within us. Don't look too much to human beings as the final word.

The Creator made natural laws for this world. The same sun rises and sets on the Buddhist and the Christian and the Indian. There are laws that govern the human world we experience, and there are different laws that operate in the spirit world. We don't have a word for "supernatural," for all things work according to the natural laws and natural ways of the Creator. Many things we will never understand. Our senses and our minds will never be enough to understand the Great Spirit, which is bigger than the universe and smaller than the atom. That is why my people call the Creator the Great Mystery.

There are also natural consequences of the natural laws, and there is no getting around them. If we are out of balance it may mean turmoil or a lack of self-esteem or other troubles in our lives. If we put out anger and fear, that is what we will get back. We are starting to see the consequences of when people say they honor the Creator but have no respect for his creation, when they go against the natural laws.

So we begin our spiritual walk, and the tree within us begins to grow. There are still many places where we will stumble into a hole or get stuck in a place. But if we are real within ourselves, if we look honestly at ourselves and begin to change the ways we are out of balance, we will begin to fill in the holes; we can pick ourselves up and begin to walk once more. The Red Road is not an easy one to travel, and I tell people that I'm not doing them any favors by showing them these ways. But when we make changes regularly and every day try to maintain that conscious contact with the Creator, we begin to have a spiritual awakening. It is not a sudden thing, like you get a flash and suddenly you're a perfect person. But added up through the days, these changes and these spiritual experiences result in the spiritual awakening that is our new life. It is a constant becoming of what we always were, what we were always meant to be. We do not seek perfection, because we are still human and are not perfect. Instead we seek balance. Things begin to fall into place; we feel a serenity and a peace with those around us and with the animals and the trees and the whole Creation.

Sometimes my people speak of a Great Weaver in the Sky that weaves together our dreams and our life and our fate, and as we find balance we begin to see the patterns of our life. We begin to see the whole blanket that is woven, the threads and the lives that are all woven together. Yet even when we see the patterns, when we have begun to fill in the holes and we think we know where we are headed and have set goals for ourselves, there will still be many surprises along the way. There will be new people in our lives; there will be new joy and new suffering. Yet with the invisible shield we have and our conscious contact with the Creator we will find the strength we need to endure, we can still remain in the balance.

So how will we know if we are following the will of Tunkashila? My grandfather said that if our thoughts and emotions, our words and actions are all one and are of service to the People, then we are doing the will of the Creator. And the People can include the four-footed people, the winged people, the trees, which we call the "standing praying people"—because all these are our relatives. The path that we walk in this life is but a small circle within the greater circle of life. In that Sacred Circle all things are related, and we are connected to all things within the circle. Nothing is better than or more holy. Each of us is just one of the Creator's many children, but as children of holy parents we have responsibilities that we must try to fulfill.

In the old days everything was done for the good of the tribe, for the People. In many ways it was a necessary part of survival, as when the people worked together for a good buffalo hunt. If one person went out alone and scattered the herds, it could ruin it for everyone and all might starve. If the hunt was successful, then the chiefs made sure that first the elders and the orphans and the poor had meat. That was the way of our chiefs. A chief was one who put the people before himself and had the trust of the people. Our chiefs were often poor because they gave everything away. We had our hereditary chiefs, too, but unless they had the hearts and the trust of the people, they had no following. Many times my grandfather would say that you are what the People say you are, not what you say you are. If you work only for yourself, doesn't that mean you think you are better than the People?

You hear a lot of the idea in the dominant culture that the individual is everything, and that freedom means I can do whatever I think is right as long as it doesn't hurt anyone. With us it's a little different, because everything is for the group; it's a different kind of freedom. I must be strong within myself so that I may have something to give to the tribe, to the People. My grandfather said that you can't give something you don't have, and a chief can be a chief only if he has something to give. And my elders always taught that we must give if we take something, or when something is given to us. In the Native American culture we "give away" when we are honored, say, with the birth of a child, or to show our sorrow at the passing on of a loved one. Sometimes people will give away everything they have. But in the circle of giving they will receive back the things they need. It is the same way when we pray for others.

As you begin to find balance and walk your spiritual walk, the walk gets a little stronger and a little stronger; it becomes a part of everything you do. And so you take it to your family and the people around you, because you are something of a messenger now. We don't go around proselytizing or trying to convert anyone to anything; but those that are there are there so that they can bring a balance and be of service to their people.

When a person pledges the Sun Dance or carries the Sacred Pipe, he or she is making a commitment to be in service to the People and must look to be a comforter instead of wanting always to be comforted. Sometimes the pipe can be a heavy thing to carry, but we try to live in this way, to seek the balance and have something to give to the People. Sometimes when I am pouring the water in the Purification Lodge and it's all Indians in there, I'll talk about the ancestors that we honor, our great leaders and warriors, like Crazy Horse and Geronimo and Chief Joseph, but I remind them that we also are the ancestors. We are the ancestors to those yet unborn, and to all the generations to come. And this is how we must live, so we will be honored for the good things that we leave for the generations to come.

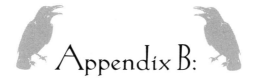

# Appendix B:

# IN THE LODGE OF PURIFICATION

*Louis never presented himself as an authority on the ceremonies of his people, but to him the Lodge of Purification (a term he always preferred over "sweat lodge") was the foundation of his people's spiritual ways. The following is a composite of some of the things he spoke of concerning his deep respect for the Purification Lodge.*

When you come into this lodge you should know that this isn't a place we come to get hot. This is our church, a church that is thousands and thousands of years old. It's not a fancy church with a big steeple; we can't impress the Creator with such things. It's just some willows and some blankets, but all these things have meaning to us. We show respect for the things the Creator has made: the rocks, the fire, the water, the air we breathe. We don't collect money to build this church, but we all share in the work of putting up the lodge and getting the wood and keeping the area in a good way, keeping it as a sacred place.

In here I am just the man who pours the water. I am no better than anyone else. Yet in our ways, the one who pours the water should be one who has earned or has been given that right. In the Sun Dance Way one must dance for four years before he or she may be given the right to pour the water. No one has been given the right to charge money for this sacred ceremony. The one who pours the water should know the songs and the ceremony and the construction of the lodge and the meanings of certain things. When you come here, come with an open mind. Do not bring your own ways and ideas in here. When I go to the lodges of other tribes I don't bring my Mandan and Lakota ways, unless they ask me to sing a song or something. I respect the ways of the one who pours the water. But inside the lodge we each pray to the one Creator in the way we know in our hearts.

When we enter the lodge we say, "Mitakuye oyasin," or "All my relations," because we are entering the Sacred Circle where all things are related as the children of one Creator. When we leave we say the same thing, because that is how we should live. When we enter we crawl in on all fours, to honor our elder relations, the animals and other creatures, for we human beings were the last to be created. We come into the circle and the door is closed, and in the darkness there is no more color of skin, there is no more impressing anyone with our fancy clothes or watch. We are all the same, just as we are in spirit. That is why there are no membership qualifications—only that we come with respect and with humbleness.

When we enter, we are entering the womb of our Mother. There is no time in here. We are going back to the beginning of creation, when all things were in the spirit. The four elements were there: the earth, the fire, the water, and the air. All life depends on these things, and we show them our respect. We call the water the "Water of Life," not to give it a fancy name, but because that is what it is. Think of how long we would survive without water. In the Sun Dance and on the fast we learn just how precious water is.

We come in here not just to sweat but to purify the physical, the emotional, the mental, and the spiritual. We bring the rocks in here, and we respect them and call them "the grandfathers," because they are ancient and because they are a part of the original creation. The rocks can teach us and tell us many things. On the rocks we pour the Water of Life, and we release the breath of the grandfather rocks to purify us.

We come into the lodge to find the balance; here we come to find a conscious contact with God, with the Creator. Into the lodge we invite the spirits to join us and to hear our prayers. Someone once asked me whether I thought that we go to the spirits or the spirits come to us. I believe that it is through humble and sincere prayers that we go to the spirits, and they hear our prayers, and sometimes they make themselves known.

In here we pray from our hearts. We pray for all people, the children, the elders, the ones who are suffering, and for the Earth, and we also pray for strength for ourselves. We are each of our own thinking, but we try to leave our "stuff" outside the lodge. If we bring it in here we must give it to the rocks. We are each of our own thinking, but we follow the path of the Sun as we go around the lodge and find the circle. We sing and we gain strength, and we give of that strength to this one and this one and this one around the circle. It starts small, but over time it gets stronger and stronger. Sometimes we like to laugh and joke in here too, and there are times for that.

We crawl into the womb of the Mother, and there we find a rebirth, we can begin again. And so when we leave, we must try to stay within the Sacred Circle. We must continue to walk our talk and walk our prayers. But with that strength we have gained we find we can go out and things don't bother us anymore. You may be driving around in traffic and someone gives you the bird, or there's someone you didn't want to see, but it doesn't ruin your day. You can stay in balance. This peace, this balance, this strength we take to our families, to our work, to all the ones around us.

So as long as there are the willows and the rocks and the water and the fire, we will have our church and our way of prayer. *Mitakuye oyasin.*